THE
ANTI-CORONARY
COOKBOOK

THE ANTI-CORONARY COOKBOOK

how to achieve weight reduction and cholesterol control

by Nathalie Havenstein
B.Sc., Cert. of Dietetics

and Elizabeth Richardson
B.Sc., Cert. of Dietetics

LUTTERWORTH PRESS
Richard Smart Publishing

Published in Great Britain 1976 by
Lutterworth Press, Luke House,
Farnham Road, Guildford, Surrey
and Richard Smart Publishing

ISBN 0 7188 7005 0

Printed by Jolly & Barber Limited
Rugby, Warwickshire

First published in Australia 1969 by
Ure Smith, Sydney, a division of
Books for Pleasure Pty Ltd

Reprinted September 1969, April 1971
July 1971, February 1972
Second edition 1974, reprinted 1975
Third edition 1976

CONTENTS

ACKNOWLEDGMENTS

The authors wish to express their appreciation to their many friends and colleagues for the generous help given in the preparation of this book. These include Dr Ralph Reader, Medical Director of the National Heart Foundation of Australia, for his continued encouragement and support for this project; Professor H. M. Whyte, and Dr P. J. Nestel, Professorial Fellow of the Department of Clinical Science, John Curtin School of Medical Research, The Australian National University, for their encouragement and constructive criticism; Dr N. A. Elvin, Clinical Superintendent and Mr A. Siddall, Food Service Manager of the Canberra Hospital for their co-operation in supplying the facilities for testing recipes; many friends who contributed their favourite recipes, in particular Mrs A. M. Chappell, Mrs P. J. Nestel and Mrs H. M. Whyte of Canberra and Miss W. Collie of Heidelberg, Victoria, and members of the Canberra Hospital and Department of Clinical Science who, in their capacity as 'official tasters', offered valuable criticism of all the tested recipes. We are especially indebted to Mrs Marilyn Horneman who so expertly devised and cooked the many recipes from which the final selection has been made and to Mrs Patsy Lucas and Mrs Paola Van Wych for their enthusiastic and accurate typing.

PUBLISHERS' NOTE

The Anti-Coronary Cookbook was first published in Australia in 1969 and has been extremely successful going into three editions and five reprints. It has also been published in America. The authors are both dietitians, Nathalie Havenstein a Research Dietitian, Department of Clinical Science, John Curtin School of Medical Research, Australian National University, Canberra, and Elizabeth Richardson, Senior Dietitian, Canberra Hospital.

The book has been very carefully prepared for publication in Great Britain and we would like to thank the British Heart Foundation, Miss R. D. Pullinger, Group Chief Dietitian, the National Heart and Chest Hospitals, Brompton Hospital, Miss Marie Jamieson, Lecturer, Department of Food Sciences, Polytechnic of North London, and Dr K. P. Ball, Central Middlesex Hospital, for their invaluable assistance.

We should like to point out that the British Heart Foundation publishes a useful series of booklets for those who suffer from diseases of the heart and circulation. They are available free from the British Heart Foundation, 57 Gloucester Place, London W1H 4DH.

FOREWORD

Today it is well known that coronary heart attacks often affect the middle-aged and this causes apprehension. Although the attack may seem unexpected – a harsh stroke of fate on victims at the peak of their careers – it can usually be traced to their previous way of living. While a few attacks may be the result of a genetic tendency, most patients have one or more of the major risk factors. These are raised blood cholesterol, cigarette smoking, and high blood pressure. Elevation of blood cholesterol levels caused by eating habits seems to be the fundamental factor leading to coronary attacks in developed countries. Where traditional ways of eating result in low cholesterol levels, cigarette smoking and high blood pressure do not lead to heart attacks. A healthy diet is therefore essential for the prevention of coronary disease.

This book explains in straightforward terms how a wife can help her husband and children develop a taste for the kind of nourishment for which nature has evolved them, rather than for much of the over-rich food to which the British public has become accustomed.

The principles of a healthier way of eating aimed at reducing the risk of heart attacks have been accepted by experts in many different countries, and have recently been emphasised by the report of the Royal College of Physicians and the British Cardiac Society on the prevention of coronary heart disease. They are:

1. *A reduction of saturated fats.*
2. *Substitution with polyunsaturated fats.*
3. *A reduction of sugar.*

Critics of the dietary approach to the prevention of heart disease often complain that doctors and dietitians should not 'mess about' with the food chosen by the British public. They forget the vast changes that have already been made in it by the use of intensive agriculture, food refining and the hydrogenation of vegetable and marine oils in the last fifty years.

Although differences of opinion among the experts have in the past led to confusion, a strong consensus of opinion now favours the approach recommended in this book. Originally written for the Australian public it has now been adapted for use here. It should do much for those who want to take a natural diet which avoids fads and fancies. It is likely to make them feel fitter and maybe live longer.

Keith Ball, MD, FRCP
Physician, Central Middlesex Hospital

INTRODUCTION

There is one main reason why this cookery book has been compiled and added to the great number of cookery books already in circulation. It is that many people are finding it difficult to adjust their cooking and eating to accord with the general principles laid down for reducing body weight and for reducing the amount of cholesterol and triglycerides in the blood without sacrificing variety, palatability and general satisfaction.

Some are patients who are overweight and have had a coronary heart attack, or a stroke, or some other evidence of disease of their arteries and they have been advised by their doctors to make these changes in their diet. Others have been similarly advised because a high level of cholesterol and/or triglycerides has been discovered in the blood or the blood pressure is high or perhaps there is a strong family history of heart disease. Still others have decided on their own initiative to make these changes in the belief, or hope, that this will protect them against this type of disease. Some may belong to a household in which one member has been advised to diet and will therefore be sharing in the dietary change as a matter of convenience.

Anyway, eating and drinking should always be made pleasurable and not taken as medicine. There are readily available books and pamphlets which explain, sometimes in considerable detail, the ways in which diet, blood fats (including cholesterol and triglycerides), body fatness (obesity) and coronary heart disease and other arterial diseases are possibly related. What is needed, however, is a comprehensive, practical book which can be the cook's constant companion in the kitchen, like any conventional cookery book, giving her a wide variety of dishes from which she can make her selections. Hence the present book.

For good nutrition the body requires a sufficiency of water, several vitamins and minerals, high quality proteins and calories. Calories are a measure of energy, and this the body is able to derive from starches and sugars, fats, proteins and alcohol. The exact amounts of the basic requirements which are needed vary according to such characteristics as the age and size of the person, work and physical activity, and whether the body is growing or tissues are being repaired after injury. Normally no conscious thought has to be given to these characteristics and eating and drinking are regulated by appetite, hunger and thirst against a background of personal and social customs. Most commonly this means eating three main meals each day with selections made from several categories of food – milk and cheese, meat, fish, eggs, legumes and nuts, fruit and vegetables, cereals, butter, margarine, and oils, and various beverages. Some, however, seem to fare perfectly well with a quite different number and timing of meals, or as vegetarians, or with other unusual dietary habits.

Why, then, should there be any thought of altering the diet? There are two 'epidemics' in our community – obesity and coronary heart disease – which have caused diet to come under scrutiny. Obesity, that is, being overweight with fatness, results from eating and drinking more calories than are needed and the excess is laid down as fat. Even a very small preponderance of dietary calories over energy expenditure, which can easily occur in these days of attractive, rich foods, motor cars and declining physical activity, can lead to gross obesity over a period of time. It is generally recognized that obesity is liable to cause discomfort and a variety of illnesses and that improvement can be brought about by diet. The key to treatment here is a reduction in the total amount of energy consumed in food and drink, that is, calories, while preserving a balanced diet in other respects.

The possible linkage between diet and coronary heart disease, strokes and other arterial diseases is not as clear, but the main facts are as follows. Several factors, so called 'risk factors', have been found to be commonly associated with the development of these diseases, three of the very important ones being high blood pressure, cigarette smoking and raised levels of blood fats. The higher the concentration of cholesterol and/or triglycerides in the blood, the greater the risk of developing disease. These blood fats are influenced by diet and drugs. Both the cholesterol in the diet and the quality of the fats and oils play important roles. Most of the ordinary animal fats in the diet are relatively hard at room temperature because they contain a high proportion of saturated fats; these cause the blood cholesterol and triglycerides to increase. Polyunsaturated fats which are soft at room temperature are found in fish, nuts and most vegetable oils; they cause the blood cholesterol to fall. Most of us have become accustomed to diets that are likely to raise the levels of blood cholesterol and triglycerides which may cause arterial damage over the years. There are some grounds for believing that this chain of events may be reversed or prevented by reducing the content of cholesterol and saturated fat in the diet and by increasing the consumption of polyunsaturated fat. In addition, since carbohydrates and alcohol also affect the plasma triglycerides in most people refined sugars and alcohol should not be taken in excess.

GENERAL NOTES

TESTED MEASUREMENTS FOR COOKERY

Standard metric measuring cup and spoons were used for all recipes in this book. All measures are level.

1 metric cup = 250 ml (8 fl oz) **N.B. British measuring**
1 tablespoon = 20 ml   **cup = 10 fl oz**
1 teaspoon   =   5 ml

Biscuit crumbs	1 cup	110 g $(3\frac{3}{4}$ oz)
Breadcrumbs—dry	1 cup	125 g (4 oz)
—soft	1 cup	60 g (2 oz)
Flour—plain or self-raising	1 cup	125 g (4 oz)
—wholemeal	1 cup	135 g $(4\frac{1}{3}$ oz)
Margarine	1 cup	250 g (8 oz)
Milk—powdered non fat	1 cup	80 g $(2\frac{2}{3}$ oz)
Rice—long grain raw	1 cup	200 g $(6\frac{1}{3}$ oz)
Sugar—granulated	1 cup	250 g (8 oz)
—castor	1 cup	220 g (7 oz)
—icing	1 cup	175 g $(5\frac{2}{3}$ oz)
—brown firmly packed	1 cup	170 g $(5\frac{1}{2}$ oz)
Cornflour	1 tablespoon	10 g $(\frac{1}{3}$ oz)
Custard Powder	1 tablespoon	10 g $(\frac{1}{3}$ oz)
Flour—plain or self-raising	1 tablespoon	10 g $(\frac{1}{3}$ oz)
Gelatine—powdered	1 tablespoon	12 g $(\frac{1}{2}$ oz)
Jam	1 tablespoon	25 g $(\frac{3}{4}$ oz)
Margarine	1 tablespoon	20 g $(\frac{2}{3}$ oz)
Nuts—chopped	1 tablespoon	10 g $(\frac{1}{3}$ oz)
Salt	1 tablespoon	20 g $(\frac{2}{3}$ oz)
Sugar—granulated	1 tablespoon	20 g $(\frac{2}{3}$ oz)
—castor	1 tablespoon	20 g $(\frac{2}{3}$ oz)
—icing	1 tablespoon	15 g $(\frac{1}{2}$ oz)
—brown	1 tablespoon	15 g $(\frac{1}{2}$ oz)
Yeast—dried	1 tablespoon	10 g $(\frac{1}{3}$ oz)
—compressed	1 tablespoon	20 g $(\frac{2}{3}$ oz)

Specific oven temperatures have not been stated in any of the recipes in this book. Oven temperatures vary with the site of the elements in electric ovens. The oven used for testing these recipes was an electric oven.

For electric ovens the suggested range may be:

	°C	°F
Hot	230–290	450–550
Moderate	180–220	350–425
Slow	140–160	275–325

For gas ovens the suggested range may be:

	Gas mark
Hot	6–8
Moderate	3–5
Slow	$\frac{1}{4}$–2

I
THE MODIFIED FAT DIET

The following five sections give the general principles which apply in this type of diet, some information about polyunsaturated fats which are available on the market and then details of the kinds and quantities of foods which may be eaten when following a Strict Modified Fat Diet. The strict diet is for use by those who have been strongly advised by their doctor to make these changes so as to lower their blood cholesterol and triglycerides. Others will probably choose to be more flexible in their adherence to the general theme of the diet. Later, hints are given at the beginning of each section of recipes to help with shopping as well as with the preparation and cooking of dishes and, finally, an example of a week's menu has been given to demonstrate the variety of meals which can be achieved.

GENERAL PRINCIPLES OF THE DIET

1.   Restrict the consumption of egg yolk, animal fats, organ meats, e.g. liver, kidneys, brains and sweetbreads, roe, oysters, lobster, prawns and crayfish. These are high in cholesterol.

2.   Restrict the consumption of butter, cream, full cream milk, animal fats, foods containing lard, dripping, chicken fat, 'hard' margarines, coconut fat and coconut, commercially prepared cakes, biscuits and pies. These are rich in 'saturated' fats which tend to raise the blood cholesterol and triglyceride levels (the blood fats). 'Saturated' or 'hard' fats are those which usually become solid or hard when cold.

3.   Increase the consumption of seed oils and 'soft' or polyunsaturated margarines. Polyunsaturated fat tends to lower the blood cholesterol and triglyceride levels. Vegetable fats which remain in their 'soft' or oil form when cold may be predominantly mono-unsaturated, as with olive oil, or polyunsaturated, as with safflower oil and others mentioned later. It is the polyunsaturated fats which are

important in this diet and to obtain maximum benefit the amount of polyunsaturated fat eaten each day should be at least one and a half times the amount of saturated fat.

4.   Restrict the use of sugar and refined carbohydrates, e.g. jam, honey, syrups, soft drinks, lollies. In some people these foods caused a marked rise in the level of blood triglycerides. The blood triglyceride level is also raised by alcohol and by saturated fats and is particularly sensitive to any increase in body weight above ideal body weight (see page 97). It is very important not to increase your weight. Remember that fats supply twice as many calories as proteins and carbohydrates, and slightly more than alcohol. If the fat in the diet is increased, the daily intake of proteins, carbohydrates and/or alcohol, especially beer, will have to restricted. If you are overweight then weight reduction can be combined with this Modified Fat Diet (see Restricted Calorie Diet II, p. 98).

2

POLYUNSATURATED OILS, MARGARINES AND MAYONNAISE

POLYUNSATURATED OILS AND MARGARINE

The seed oils, safflower, sunflower, soybean, corn or maize oils have a high content of polyunsaturated fats. Safflower oil has the highest content of any commonly available oil. Peanut oil has a moderately low content of polyunsaturated fat, while olive has a very low content and for this reason these two oils are not recommended for use in the Modified Fat Diet. The recommended oils may be purchased in most supermarkets or grocery stores. Bulk purchases are usually cheaper.

Polyunsaturated margarines are those margarines which have a high content of polyunsaturated fats in the finished product. These margarines are produced by special manufacturing processes whereby the polyunsaturated nature of the fat is preserved whereas in most margarines any polyunsaturated fats present in the raw material are largely converted to saturated and mono-unsaturated fats during the process of manufacture. The following products are therefore suitable for use in the Modified Fat Diet – corn oil, sunflower seed oil, safflower seed oil, Mazola, Spry Crisp 'n' Dry, Trex vegetable oil, and Flora margarine.

POLYUNSATURATED MAYONNAISE AND DRESSINGS

Alfonal mayonnaise is suitable for use in the Modified Fat Diet. This product contains a negligible amount of cholesterol. Kraft and Heinz French and Kraft Italian Dressings are suitable for use in the Modified Fat Diet.

3
THE STRICT MODIFIED FAT DIET

Guide-lines are given to indicate the quantities and types of foods which may be eaten each day when following this diet. Foods which are high in saturated fats and cholesterol have been reduced but not entirely eliminated from this diet because this may involve unacceptably extreme changes in eating habits. To avoid putting on weight there may need to be a restriction in such foods as sugar, cakes, desserts, confectionery and high calorie beverages to compensate for the increased consumption of calories from fat in the form of margarine and oil.

The amounts of margarine, oil, meat, milk and eggs (fat and cholesterol containing foods) outlined in the following diets are examples of the amounts of these foods which when included as part of a 2000 Calorie or 2500 Calorie diet would meet dietary recommendations.

FATS

	2000 kcals	2500 kcals
Polyunsaturated margarine	6 tsp (30 g)	2 tbsp (40 g)
Polyunsaturated oil	5 tsp (25 ml)	5 tsp (25 ml)

MEATS

	2000 kcals	2500 kcals
Chicken, rabbits, fish	100 g (3½ oz)	150 g (5 oz)
Lean lamb, beef	75 g (2½ oz)	90 g (3 oz)

No more than 8 servings of lamb, beef per week. Use equivalent amounts of chicken or fish or cheese substitution, 30 g (1 oz) cheese = 30 g lamb or beef, for other meals.

MILK

	2000 kcals	2500 kcals
Skim milk	300 ml (10 fl oz)	450 ml (15 fl oz)

Non-fat dry skim milk powder, buttermilk or non-fat yoghurt may also be used.

EGGS

Up to 3 egg *yolks*   Up to 3 egg *yolks*
per week   per week

Egg *white* is unrestricted.

CHEESE

Cottage cheese is unrestricted because it is the only cheese which does not contain butterfat. Creamed cottage cheese contains a small amount of butterfat. All other cheeses contain butterfat and may only be used when substituted for lamb or beef, 30 g (1 oz) = 30 g (1 oz) meat. Do not use more than 125 g (4 oz) per week.

VEGETABLES
*FRUIT AND FRUIT
JUICES
BREAD AND CEREALS
*ALCOHOL
CONFECTIONERY
(exclude chocolate, fudges, caramels)

These foods do not contain saturated fat or cholesterol and may be eaten according to calorie requirement

*CAKES, BISCUITS, PASTRIES

Home made items using polyunsaturated fats and oils and including no more than the equivalent of three egg yolks per week are permitted. See further details in sections Cakes and Biscuits (page 61) and Desserts (page 69). It is best not to eat commercially prepared products because the exact ingredients are unknown.

Remember—if blood triglyceride levels are high then the intake of foods marked * must be reduced. If you are overweight and have high blood cholesterol and triglycerides then the *total intake of calories* as well as cholesterol, sugars, alcohol and saturated fats must all be restricted until you attain your Desirable Weight (see page 97). For Special Weight Reduction Diet see Energy Restricted Diet No. 2 (page 99).

The following may be used freely as desired – tea, coffee, low calorie soft drinks, essences, herbs, spices, vinegar.

Full cream milk in all forms, e.g., pasteurized, homogenized, evaporated, condensed or dried
Cream, butter, animal fats, i.e. lard, dripping
All cheeses except cottage cheese
Extra egg yolks
Fatty bacon, except lean back bacon
Sausages
'Hard' margarine, palm and coconut oils, coconut, chocolate
Organ meats, i.e. brains, kidneys, liver and sweetbreads
Fish roe, caviar

These foods are rich sources of cholesterol and/or saturated fat and should be eliminated from your diet.

WHEN DINING OUT

Select fruit juice or fruit cocktails, non-creamed soups, grills (especially fish), salads, fruit or gelatine desserts and water ices. Avoid sauces and salad dressings made with butter or cream. Ask for desserts to be served without cream.

4

INTRODUCTION TO RECIPES FOR MODIFIED FAT DIET

The recipes included in the following sections illustrate how polyunsaturated margarines and oils may be substituted for the saturated cooking fats, i.e. dripping, lard, butter, ghee or ordinary margarines.

Most of these recipes are for simple every-day dishes. A few of the more exotic dishes have been included for use on special occasions. By a few simple alterations your own favourite recipes may be adapted to suit the Modified Fat Diet.

If this Modified Diet is to be maximally effective then *at least one and a half times as much polyunsaturated fat as saturated fat needs to be eaten.* It is for this reason that the amount of polyunsaturated margarines or oil included in some of these recipes is probably more than you would normally use. To ascertain how much of the polyunsaturated margarine or oil each member of the family will get from a particular dish it is necessary to divide the quantity of polyunsaturated margarine or oil by the number of servings. This has been done for most recipes, e.g. Per serve: 2 teaspoons oil.

Egg yolk is very high in cholesterol. Because of this the number of whole eggs per recipe has been limited to one. No restriction is placed on the number of egg whites used.

5
RECIPES FOR MODIFIED FAT DIET

SOUPS

Occasionally tinned and packet soups may be used provided skim milk, buttermilk or low fat yoghurt is used as the reconstituting fluid when the directions call for milk or cream. When preparing stock from meat, cook the stock the day before it is required and chill. After removal of all fat, proceed according to the recipe.

Do not use cream either in the preparation or as a garnish.

Favourite recipes may be adapted by substituting polyunsaturated margarine or oil for butter, when sautéing vegetables or making the white sauce bases for soups.

Garnishes such as croutons, garlic, parsley or herb breads may be used in order to increase the amount of polyunsaturated fats eaten each day.

BASIC CREAM SOUP

2 tablespoons polyunsatured margarine
2 tablespoons plain flour
½ teaspoon salt
pinch cayenne pepper
½ pint skim milk
¼ cup polyunsaturated oil
½ pint vegetable stock (liquid in which vegetables
were cooked)

METHOD

1. Melt margarine in saucepan and remove from hotplate
2. Add flour, salt and pepper and stir with a wooden spoon until smooth
3. Stir over heat 1 minute; do not brown
4. Add milk all at once stirring constantly until it boils and thickens
5. Gradually add oil, beating well
6. Stir in vegetable stock until it is well blended

7. To this soup, add sieved cooked carrots, peas, cauliflower, onions, spinach, pumpkin, tomato purée, or asparagus. If preferred, vegetables may be left in small pieces
8. Garnish with croutons (p. 87) and parsley

N.B. Garlic bread (p. 90), herb bread (p. 90) or parsley bread (p. 90) may be served with soup

Per serve: 5 teaspoons oil equivalent   Serves 4

CHILLED TOMATO SOUP

425 g (15 fl oz) canned tomato juice
½ pint buttermilk or low fat yoghurt
1 tablespoon lemon juice
few drops Tabasco sauce
150 ml (5 fl oz) skim milk (optional)
1 tablespoon finely sliced shallots
Finely chopped parsley

METHOD

1. Combine tomato juice with buttermilk or yoghurt, lemon juice, sauce and shallots
2. Stir in skim milk. Chill. Sprinkle with parsley before serving   Serves 4

CHINESE CHICKEN SOUP

125 g (4 oz) raw chicken cut into strips
1 teaspoon salt
1 tablespoon cornflour
2 tablespoons cold water
4 cups chicken stock
2 teaspoons soy sauce
4 fresh mushrooms skinned and sliced
1 tablespoon polyunsatured oil
1 tablespoon lemon juice

METHOD

1. Sprinkle chicken strips with salt and set aside
2. Blend cornflour with cold water and add to stock. Add soy sauce
3. Bring to the boil, stirring constantly
4. Add chickens strips and simmer for 5 minutes

5. Heat oil in pan and sauté mushrooms for 5 minutes
6. Add mushrooms and lemon juice to soup. Simmer for 5 minutes

Per serve: 1 teaspoon oil · Serves 4

CREOLE VEGETABLE SOUP

1 tablespoon chopped onion
1 tablespoon polyunsaturated oil
2 cups chicken stock
1 teaspoon mixed herbs
1 cup canned tomatoes
¼ cup cooked fresh or frozen corn or
whole kernel canned corn
1 level tablespoon uncooked rice
Salt and pepper to taste

METHOD

1. Sauté onions in oil in large saucepan. Add all ingredients
2. Bring to boil, cover and simmer for 20 minutes
3. Serve with croutons (p. 87)

Per serve: 1 teaspoon oil · Serves 4

FISH CHOWDER

2 cups boiling water
1½ teaspoons salt
500 g (1 lb) fish fillets
100 ml (3 fl oz) polyunsaturated oil
¼ cup chopped onion
1 cup diced raw potato
Dash pepper
1 tablespoon chopped parsley
2 cups skim milk
2 tablespoons flour

METHOD

1. Bring salted water to boil and add fish. Simmer for 15–20 minutes (do not boil). Reserve stock
2. Cook onions in half the oil until transparent

3. Add potatoes, pepper and fish stock. Boil 15 minutes or until potatoes are tender. Add flaked fish and parsley
4. Blend flour with skim milk and add to fish mixture
5. Allow mixture to boil, remove from hotplate and gradually add the remainder of the oil

Per serve: 1½ tablespoons oil   Serves 4

FRENCH ONION SOUP

3 tablespoons polyunsaturated oil
2 cups finely chopped onion
4 cups beef stock
Salt and pepper to taste

METHOD

1. Sauté onions in oil until golden
2. Add stock, seasonings and simmer ½ hour
3. Serve with croutons (p. 87)

Per serve: 3 teaspoons oil   Serves 4

FISH

Fish is a food which contains very little saturated fat. One serving of fish contains less saturated fat than the equivalent serving of lamb, mutton, pork or beef. For this reason it is recommended that fish be included in the family menu several times each week.

All types of fish are suitable, i.e. fresh and frozen fillets, smoked and salted fish such as kippers and canned fish such as tuna, salmon and fish canned in oils, e.g. sardines.

Do not eat fish roe, which is high in cholesterol.

Do not buy fish fingers, fish cakes, etc., because you do not know how much fat or what kind of fat they contain. Commercially prepared fried fish and chips are best avoided.

The amount of polyunsaturated fat per serving can be increased by the use of polyunsaturated oils and margarines in cooking; by the addition of garnishes such as tartare sauce, parsley spread, etc.; by using fried breadcrumbs as toppings and by serving side dishes of salads with polyunsaturated dressings or mayonnaises.

BAKED FISH

750 g–1 kg (1½–2 lb) whole fish (bream, salmon
or trout)
Lemon juice
1 cup soft white breadcrumbs
Salt and pepper
Sprinkle nutmeg
2 tablespoons chopped parsley
3 tablespoons polyunsaturated oil

METHOD

1. Thoroughly wipe the cleaned fish, cut off fins and trim tail, remove eyes
2. Rub inside and outside of fish with lemon
3. Mix breadcrumbs with a little salt, pepper, nutmeg, chopped parsley and moisten with oil
4. Place about half this mixture inside fish and fasten fish together with skewers or sew
5. Brush large piece of foil with oil, place fish and remaining seasoning on this and seal securely
6. Place in baking dish and bake in moderate oven for 30 minutes

Serves 4

VARIATION

Omit seasoning
Season well with lemon juice, salt and pepper
Brush liberally with oil
Cook as above

Per serve: 1 tablespoon oil

BARBECUED FISH

3 tablespoons polyunsaturated oil
½ cup diced onion
750 g (1½ lb) fish fillets
Salt and pepper
1 cup barbecue sauce (p. 79)
2 tablespoons lemon juice
3 tablespoons water
1 tablespoon sugar
2 tablespoons Worcestershire sauce
½ teaspoon prepared mustard

METHOD

1. Heat oil in frypan, fry onion until brown then remove
2. Cut fillets into serving size pieces and fry until lightly browned
3. Spread onion over fish, season with salt and pepper
4. Combine barbecue sauce with other ingredients and pour over fish
5. Cover and simmer until fish is cooked

Per serve: 1 tablespoon oil   Serves 4

FISH BALLS

1 cup cooked flaked fish or canned fish
2 cups mashed potatoes
2 tablespoons polyunsaturated oil
Salt and pepper
1 egg white
Plain flour or dry breadcrumbs
Polyunsaturated oil for frying

METHOD

1. Combine fish, mashed potato, oil, salt and pepper
2. Add egg white and beat well
3. Shape into balls, toss in flour or breadcrumbs and deep fry in hot oil until brown

Per serve: 2 teaspoons minimum   Makes 18 balls

FISH CASSEROLE

500 g (1 lb) tomatoes
60 g (2 oz) polyunsaturated margarine
1 cup sliced onion
Salt and pepper
$\frac{1}{2}$ teaspoon paprika
750 g (1$\frac{1}{2}$ lb) fish fillets
Chopped parsley

METHOD

1. Skin and chop tomatoes
2. Heat half margarine and sauté onions until tender
3. Add the tomatoes and cook until well blended
4. Add paprika and season to taste

5. Cut fish fillets in 4 portions
6. Grease shallow casserole dish with remainder of margarine and place fish in dish, add sauce, parsley and cover
7. Place in moderate oven and bake for 10 minutes or until cooked

Per serve: 1 tablespoon oil   Serves 4

FISH PIE WITH HERBS

3 cups cooked flaked fish
1½ cups coating white sauce (p. 83)
2 tablespoons polyunsaturated mayonnaise
1 tablespoon chopped parsley
Salt, pepper, grated nutmeg
1 tablespoon crushed dry tarragon
1 tablespoon chopped walnuts

METHOD

1. Stir fish into white sauce, add mayonnaise and parsley. Season with salt, pepper, nutmeg
2. Put into fireproof dish and top with tarragon and walnuts
3. Brown in moderate oven

Per serve: 1½ tablespoons oil equivalent   Serves 4

GRILLED MARINADED FISH

1 clove garlic
½ cup polyunsaturated oil
3 tablespoons white vinegar or dry white wine or lemon juice
Chopped parsley
Salt and pepper
750 g (1½ lb) fish – use whole flat fish, split fish steaks or fillets

METHOD

1. Rub shallow pan or dish with garlic, add oil, vinegar, chopped parsley, salt and pepper and mix
2. Place fish in this marinade
3. Allow to marinade 15 minutes, turn and marinade another 15 minutes
4. Arrange fish on griller, grill until cooked. Brush with marinade to prevent drying

5. Serve with heated marinade poured over fish

Serves 4

VARIATION

Grilled fish with Italian dressing: Substitute $\frac{1}{2}$ cup Italian dressing for above marinade

Per serve: $1\frac{1}{2}$ tablespoons oil

POACHED FISH

750 g (1½ lb) fish
1½ teaspoons salt
2 cups water
½ cup onion rings
6 peppercorns
2 bay leaves
1 tablespoon lemon juice
1 tablespoon vinegar

METHOD

1. Cut fish into serving pieces and rub with salt
2. Place fish in pan, add water, onion and seasonings
3. Bring to boil, cover and simmer for about 20 minutes or until fish is cooked
4. Serve with horseradish sauce (p. 83), caper dressing (p. 83), tartare sauce (p. 81) or parsley sauce (p. 83)

Serves 4

PSARI PLAKI

¾ cup diced onions
2 cups diced potato
1½ cups diced carrots
¾ cup diced celery
1 cup diced tomatoes
100 ml (3 fl oz) polyunsaturated oil
750 g (1½ lb) fish fillets
Salt and pepper
Juice ½ lemon

METHOD

1. Vegetables are to be diced into pieces of the same size
2. Heat oil in frying pan and sauté vegetables

3. Place fish in greased shallow casserole dish, sprinkle with salt, pepper and lemon juice. Place vegetables and oil around and over fish
4. Cover with lid or greaseproof paper and bake in moderate oven for 30 minutes or longer if necessary

Per serve: 5 teaspoons oil   Serves 4

ROLLED FISH FILLETS
AND ANCHOVY SAUCE

750 g (1½ lb) fish fillets
Lemon
Seasoned flour
Skim milk
Dried breadcrumbs
Polyunsaturated oil

METHOD

1. Wash and dry fillets and rub with lemon
2. Roll up and secure with a toothpick
3. Coat with flour, dip in skim milk and toss in breadcrumbs
4. Deep fry in oil until a golden brown and serve with anchovy sauce (p. 83)

Per serve: 1 tablespoon oil   Serves 4

SALMON WIZZ

2 cups cooked flaked salmon
1 cup cooked peas
2 cups coating white sauce (p. 83)
Fried breadcrumbs (p. 90)

METHOD

1. Add salmon and peas to white sauce and heat, place in casserole
2. Sprinkle with fried breadcrumbs, and place in moderate oven for 10–15 minutes

Per serve: 5 teaspoons oil   Serves 4

½ cup soft breadcrumbs
2 tablespoons grated onion
1 tablespoon chopped parsley
¼ teaspoon basil
½ teaspoon salt
½ clove garlic cut finely
3 tablespoons water
750 g (1½ lb) fish fillets
3 tablespoons polyunsaturated oil

METHOD

1. Mix breadcrumbs, onion, parsley, basil, salt and garlic in small bowl
2. Moisten these ingredients with half the water and spread over fish fillets
3. Roll up fillets, securing with toothpicks and place close together in shallow baking dish
4. Pour remainder of water into bottom of dish and brush tops of rolls with oil
5. Bake in moderate oven for 20–30 minutes

Per serve: 1 tablespoon oil   Serves 4

SWEET AND SOUR TUNA

425 g (15 oz) can pineapple pieces
3 tablespoons polyunsaturated oil
1 cup sliced celery
1 cup thinly sliced carrots
125 g (4 oz) sliced mushrooms, or
125 g (4 oz) tin button mushrooms (optional)
¾ cup chopped red or green peppers
1½ cups chicken stock
3 tablespoons vinegar
1 tablespoon soy sauce (more if desired)
¼ cup sugar
3 tablespoons cornflour
½ teaspoon salt
½ teaspoon pepper
425 g (15 oz) can tuna

1. Drain pineapple, reserve ½ cup juice
2. Heat oil and sauté celery, carrots, mushrooms and peppers. Remove from pan
3. Add pineapple juice, vinegar, soy sauce to stock in saucepan and stir in sugar, cornflour, salt and pepper
4. Bring to boil stirring constantly until mixture thickens slightly
5. Add cooked vegetables and tuna. Heat thoroughly, stirring occasionally

Per serve: 3 teaspoons oil   Serves 4

VARIATIONS

Other meats or fish may be substituted for the tuna in this recipe
Sweet and sour fish: Use fried fish pieces in batter
Sweet and sour chicken: Use crumbed chicken pieces
Sweet and sour veal: Use crumbed veal pieces

MEATS

Meats are one of the major sources of animal fats in the diet and animal fats are rich in saturated fats.

All visible fat must be removed from the meat prior to cooking. Even so there still remains a large amount of fat which is an integral part of the meat and is invisible.

No more than one serving of meats rich in fat such as lamb or beef should be eaten each day. Veal has very little fat and may be eaten both in larger quantities and more frequently. Pork and all pig products have a very high fat content and may be eaten only occasionally.

HINTS ON BUYING MEATS

Always buy the lean cuts of meat, and those which are not 'marbled'.
Beef: Buy cuts which are either lean or from which the fat is easily removed, such as rump, fillet, round, topside, silverside or chuck beef. Avoid cuts such as rolled roast, blade, porterhouse or T bone steak where fat is distributed throughout the meat and cannot be removed.

Lamb: Buy the lean cuts such as leg, chump chops and shanks. Loin chops and cutlets may be used very occasionally but all fat must be cut off before cooking.

Avoid cuts such as shoulder and breast or flaps. These are usually very fatty.

Veal: All cuts are suitable.

Pork: All cuts of pork have a high content of fat and therefore consumption of pork must be severely restricted. Buy only the leanest cuts such as leg, loin and chump chops. If buying ham choose the leanest cuts, e.g. leg ham, avoiding rolled or shoulder hams.

Miscellaneous: Do not buy fat bacon or sausages. Tongue, tripe and lean back bacon may be eaten if desired.

When you require minced meat, either ask your butcher to mince specially selected and trimmed round or topside or else do your own mincing at home. Do not buy pre-minced meat from the butcher because you cannot be sure of its fat content. For the same reason avoid buying sausages and sausage mince.

When you have chosen your meat ask your butcher to trim away all visible fat.

COOKING MEAT FOR THE MODIFIED FAT DIET

1. Remove all visible fat when preparing meat for cooking.
2. Use only polyunsaturated margarine or oil in cooking. Brush oil or margarine over meat prior to grilling.
3. Whenever possible braises, casseroles and stews should be cooked the day before use and cooled. The fat will then rise to the top and solidify and can easily be removed.
4. When roasting meat place it on a rack in baking dish. Always use polyunsaturated oil or margarine as the basting agent and *not* the meat drippings which contain the saturated fats.
5. When grilling meat always place it on a rack so that the drippings may drain away from the meat. If using an electric frypan always tilt pan so that the fat drains away from the meat.
6. If meat is marinaded the marinade may be used for basting the meat during cooking.

BEEF IN BURGUNDY

500 g (1 lb) lean topside steak
2 cups sliced onion
Thyme, parsley, bay leaf
2½ cups burgundy
1 clove garlic
2 tablespoons flour
100 ml (3 fl oz) polyunsaturated oil
125 g (4 oz) sliced mushrooms
1 dozen small onions or 3 large onions quartered

METHOD

1. Trim all fat and cut meat into bite-size pieces and place in an earthenware dish
2. Season with salt and pepper, cover with 1 cup sliced onions, few sprigs thyme and parsley tied together, bay leaf, half polyunsaturated oil, and burgundy. Leave to marinade for 3 hours
3. Heat remaining oil in pan, brown remaining sliced onions and remove
4. Add drained pieces of meat to pan, reserving liquid, and brown quickly
5. Add flour, cook for one minute then add strained liquid from marinade. Allow to boil and thicken
6. Add chopped garlic, herbs, cover tightly and gently simmer for 2 hours
7. Add small onions, mushrooms and cook a further half hour

Per serve: 5 teaspoons oil　　　　　　　　Serves 4

BRAISED STEAK

3 tablespoons polyunsaturated oil
500 g (1 lb) lean round steak cut into squares
2 cups carrot rings
1 cup sliced celery
1½ cups parsnip rings
1½ cups onion rings
Salt and pepper
4 tablespoons tomato sauce
1 tablespoon soy sauce
1 tablespoon Worcestershire sauce
2 cups beef stock

38

METHOD

1. Heat oil, add meat and brown well
2. Arrange ingredients in a greased casserole dish. First the meat then vegetables and salt and pepper
3. Mix stock with tomato, soy and Worcestershire sauces
4. Pour stock over meat and vegetables, and bake in moderate oven 2–2½ hours

Per serve: 3 teaspoons oil   Serves 4

BRAISED VEAL CHOPS

4 large veal chops
2 tablespoons polyunsaturated oil
2 cups onion rings
½ cup red pepper cut in thin strips
1½ cups skinned and chopped tomatoes
Salt and pepper
2 tablespoons chopped parsley

METHOD

1. Trim chops, remove all fat
2. Heat oil in pan, add chops and onions and cook slowly for a few minutes to brown
3. Add red pepper and tomatoes, season with salt and pepper
4. Cover, cook slowly, approximately 25 minutes or until chops are tender

Per serve: 2 teaspoons oil   Serves 4

MADRAS DRY CURRY

100 ml (3 fl oz) polyunsaturated oil
1 cup chopped onions
2 cloves finely sliced garlic
1 tablespoon curry powder
2 tablespoons tamarind purée or paste
(if unavailable substitute 1 tablespoon plum jam
combined with 1 tablespoon lemon juice)
500 g (1 lb) lean chuck steak cut into cubes
Salt

1. Heat oil, fry onion and garlic until golden
2. Add curry powder, mix thoroughly then add tamarind purée or paste and meat
3. Cover, simmer 1½–2 hours or until meat is tender
4. Add salt to taste

Per serve: 1½ tablespoons oil   Serves 4

MALAYSIAN LAMB CURRY

750 g (1½ lb) lean lamb chump chops
100 ml (3 fl oz) polyunsaturated oil
1¼ cups diced onions
2 cloves garlic
½ pt buttermilk or low fat yoghurt
¼–½ teaspoon chilli sauce or powder
½ teaspoon turmeric
1¼ tablespoons curry powder
Salt

METHOD

1. Cut meat into bite-size cubes
2. Place all ingredients except salt in saucepan then add meat
3. Bring to boil and simmer gently until meat is tender
4. Season to taste with salt. Serve with boiled rice

Per serve: 1½ tablespoons oil   Serves 4

MEXICAN RICE

3 tablespoons polyunsaturated oil
½ cup uncooked rice
1 cup thinly sliced onion
1 small clove garlic, finely crushed
500 g (1 lb) lean minced chuck steak
2 teaspoons salt
3 teaspoons chilli powder or chilli sauce
4 tablespoons tomato sauce
250 g (½ lb) skinned roughly chopped tomatoes
1 cup water
¾ cup raisins

METHOD

1. Heat oil in frying pan, add rice and toss frequently until lightly browned
2. Add onion, garlic and minced steak, stirring until meat is browned. Stir in salt, chilli powder, tomato sauce, tomatoes, water and raisins
3. Cover, simmer 25 minutes (stirring occasionally) or until rice is tender

Per serve: 3 teaspoons oil   Serves 4

ROAST SEASONED VEAL

*1 thick piece veal leg, about 1.5–1.75 kg
(3–3½ lb) cut with pocket, or boned shoulder
2 teaspoons prepared mustard
90 g (3 oz) finely chopped mushrooms (optional)
¼ cup finely chopped celery
½ cup chopped onion
2 tablespoons chopped parsley
4 tablespoons soft breadcrumbs
Salt and pepper
100 ml (3 fl oz) polyunsaturated oil

METHOD

1. Spread prepared mustard inside pocket
2. Combine mushrooms, celery, onion, parsley, breadcrumbs and salt and pepper. Add 30 ml (1 fl oz) oil and blend well. Fill into pocket. Secure with skewers or string and brush with oil
3. Bake in a moderate oven; allow 20–25 minutes per pound and 25 minutes over. Baste frequently with oil
4. Serve with potatoes baked in their jackets or baked in polyunsaturated oil

Per serve: 1½ tablespoons oil   Serves 4
*Lamb leg may be substituted for veal leg

SAVOURY MINCE

½ cup grated onion
500 g (1 lb) minced lean beef
3 tablespoons polyunsaturated oil

$\frac{3}{4}$ *cup grated carrot*
$\frac{1}{2}$ *cup grated potato*
$\frac{1}{2}$ *cup chopped celery*
2 tablespoons tomato sauce
1 tablespoon Worcestershire sauce
1$\frac{1}{4}$ cups beef stock
2 tablespoons flour
Salt and pepper

METHOD

1. Fry onions and meat in oil until brown then add carrots, potato and celery
2. Mix together tomato sauce, Worcestershire sauce, stock, flour, pepper and salt until well blended and smooth
3. Add to meat mixture and simmer 30 minutes until cooked. This may be used as filling for meat pies using savoury pastry (p. 92)

Per serve: 1 tablespoon oil   Serves 4

SHREDDED VEAL AND CELERY (CHINESE STYLE)

750 g (1$\frac{1}{2}$ lb) veal steak
1 tablespoon soy sauce
2 tablespoons dry sherry
1$\frac{1}{2}$ cups chicken stock
Cornflour
Salt and pepper
3 cups sliced celery
100 ml (3 fl oz) polyunsaturated oil
1 tablespoon water

METHOD

1. Cut meat into thin strips about 5 cm (2 inches) long
2. In basin combine soy sauce, dry sherry and chicken stock; add meat, cover and stand overnight
3. Next day remove meat from marinade, drain well, reserve marinade
4. Add salt and pepper to cornflour. Toss meat in this mixture
5. Wash celery, cut into thin diagonal strips
6. Sauté veal quickly in hot oil, remove from pan, add celery and cook quickly

7. Return meat to pan with marinade. Blend 1 tablespoon cornflour with water, add to pan, stirring until sauce thickens. If too thick, add more stock

Per serve: 1½ tablespoons oil   Serves 4

SPAGHETTI WITH MEAT SAUCE

3 tablespoons polyunsaturated oil
250 g (½ lb) finely minced lean topside
¾ cup finely grated onion
2 cloves crushed garlic
500 g (1 lb) peeled chopped tomatoes
1 teaspoon oregano or basil
1 teaspoon salt
Pepper to taste
3 tablespoons tomato paste
1 cup beef stock or dry red wine
250 g (½ lb) spaghetti or macaroni
2 tablespoons polyunsaturated margarine
or garlic spread (p. 81)

METHOD

1. Heat oil in frying pan, add meat, garlic and onion. Brown lightly
2. Add chopped peeled tomatoes, oregano, salt and pepper
3. Blend tomato paste with beef stock and add to mixture
4. Simmer for 30 minutes with lid off saucepan so that sauce reduces slightly
5. When sauce is almost ready, cook spaghetti in boiling salted water
6. Drain spaghetti and place on hot serving dish or plate
7. Fold margarine or garlic spread into spaghetti
8. Pour hot meat sauce over spaghetti
9. Serve with garlic bread (p. 90)

Per serve: 1 tablespoon oil   Serves 4

STUFFED VEAL ROLLS

750 g (1½ lb) veal steak
½ cup polyunsaturated oil
¾ cup finely chopped onions
2 cups soft breadcrumbs

$\frac{3}{4}$ *cup coarsely chopped apple*
Salt and pepper to taste
2 tablespoons flour
2 cups apple juice or cider
2 tablespoons cornflour

METHOD

1. Cut veal into serving pieces, flatten out until very thin
2. Heat half the oil, add onions and sauté
3. Add breadcrumbs, apple, salt and pepper and cook 4 minutes
4. Remove and place 1 heaped tablespoon stuffing on each veal slice
5. Roll up, secure with a toothpick, roll in flour
6. Heat remaining oil and brown rolls well on both sides
7. Add apple juice or cider, cover and simmer 30–35 minutes or until tender
8. Blend cornflour with some cold apple juice and add to gravy. Stir until it boils and thickens

Per serve: 30 ml (1 fl oz)   Serves 4

VEAL GOULASH

750 g (1$\frac{1}{2}$ lb) veal
$\frac{3}{4}$ *cup sliced onions*
3 tablespoons polyunsaturated oil
1 tablespoon paprika
Salt and pepper
150 ml (5 fl oz) chicken stock
1 bay leaf
2 teaspoons lemon juice
$\frac{1}{2}$ *cup buttermilk*
1 tablespoon cornflour

METHOD

1. Cut veal into bite-size cubes
2. Soften onion in the hot oil; add the meat and brown
3. Add paprika and salt and pepper to taste and cook a little longer
4. Add the stock, bay leaf; cover pan and simmer for 1$\frac{1}{2}$ hours, stirring occasionally (add more liquid if it becomes too dry)
5. Pour lemon juice into buttermilk, add cornflour, blend and add to veal, stir until thickened

Per serve: 1 tablespoon oil   Serves 4

VEAL MARENGO

750 g (1½ lb) veal steak
½ cup seasoned flour
Salt and pepper
3 tablespoons polyunsaturated oil
1 clove crushed garlic
150 ml (5 fl oz) white wine
2 cups chicken stock
1 tablespoon tomato paste
1½ cups skinned and chopped tomatoes
1½ cups chopped onions
125 g (4 oz) sliced mushrooms
Chopped parsley

METHOD

1. Cut steak into serving size pieces; toss in seasoned flour
2. Heat oil in large frying pan, add meat and brown. Remove and place in casserole
3. Fry crushed garlic a few minutes, add remaining flour and cook, stirring occasionally until lightly browned
4. Gradually add wine and chicken stock, bring to boil. Add tomato paste and stir
5. Simmer gently until reduced by half. Pour over meat
6. Add tomatoes, onions and mushrooms to meat, cover casserole. Bake in moderate oven until tender (approximately 1½–2 hours)

Per serve: 1 tablespoon oil   Serves 4

VEAL AND POTATO CASSEROLE

750 g (1½ lb) veal
125 g (4 oz) polyunsaturated margarine
3½ cups coarsely cut onions
Salt to taste
12 whole peppercorns
2 bay leaves
4 cups diced potatoes

METHOD

1. Cut meat into cubes
2. Melt margarine in pan and turn meat and onions in it but do not brown

3. Add boiling water until the meat is just covered then
3. Add boiling water until the meat is just covered then add salt, peppercorns and bay leaves
4. Simmer for about 20 minutes
5. Add the potatoes, and let the mixture cook until the potatoes have blended with the meat broth giving the appearance of a very thick potato soup
6. Garnish with chopped chives

Per serve: 1 tablespoon oil equivalent   Serves 4

VEAL RAGOUT

750 g (1½ lb) veal
250 g (½ lb) dried apricots
½ cup polyunsaturated oil
3 cups finely chopped onions
1 clove finely sliced garlic
1 cup diced carrot
½ cup diced turnip
1 teaspoon powdered paprika
1 teaspoon curry powder
1 teaspoon saffron
1 teaspoon cinnamon
1 teaspoon cumin
1 teaspoon whole cloves
Salt, thyme and 2 bay leaves
Chicken stock

METHOD

1. Soak the apricots overnight
2. Cut the meat into bite-size cubes
3. Heat oil in a large heavy pan and brown the veal on all sides
4. Add the finely chopped onions and garlic and brown. Add carrot and turnip
5. Sprinkle salt and spices over meat and vegetables, add thyme, bay leaves, soaked apricots and apricot liquid
6. Pour sufficient stock over the meat and vegetables to cover. Cover and let mixture simmer gently for about 2½ hours

Per serve: 30 ml (1 fl oz) oil   Serves 4

POULTRY AND GAME

These meats have a low saturated fat content, and may be eaten frequently in relatively large quantities. The amount of polyunsaturated fats per serving can be greatly increased by the addition of such items as garlic or herb bread; side salads with polyunsaturated dressings or mayonnaise; or fried vegetables. Chicken and turkey do not contain as much fat per serve as duck and goose.

COOKING POULTRY AND GAME FOR THE MODIFIED FAT DIET

1. Remove any visible fat when preparing poultry for cooking. As fat lies under the skin of chicken and turkey, prick the skin before cooking to ensure that the fat drains away from the bird. Do not eat the skin.
2. Use only polyunsaturated margarine or oil in cooking. Brush oil or margarine over poultry prior to grilling.
3. When roasting poultry place it on a rack in baking dish. Always use polyunsaturated oil or margarine as the basting agent *not* the drippings which contain the saturated fats.
4. If poultry is marinaded the marinade may be used for basting the meat during cooking.

CHICKEN AND ORANGE

3 oranges
Water
1.1 kg (2½ lb) chicken
Salt, pepper
1 teaspoon paprika
60 g (2 oz) polyunsaturated margarine
2 tablespoons flour
½ tablespoon soft brown sugar
¼ teaspoon ground ginger

METHOD

1. Peel rind from one orange, remove white pith. Cut rind into fine shreds. Squeeze juice from rinded orange and one other; add water to make up to 300 ml (½ pint)
2. Divide chicken into serving portions, sprinkle with salt, pepper and paprika

3. Melt margarine in a large deep frying pan, add chicken and brown well. Remove chicken portions
4. Stir flour into pan, add sugar and ginger. Blend well. Stir in orange juice and rind. Bring to the boil, boil 2–3 minutes, adjust seasoning
5. Return chicken to sauce. Cover and simmer until chicken is tender
6. Peel third orange and divide into segments, removing membrane. Add to chicken during last 5 minutes of cooking time. Serve with plain boiled rice

Per serve: 2 teaspoons oil   Serves 4

CHICKEN AND WALNUTS

2–2½ cups uncooked chicken pieces
30 g (1 oz) dried mushrooms or
125 g (¼ lb) fresh mushrooms
¼ cup diced celery
2 teaspoons brandy or dry sherry
¼ teaspoon salt
1 clove garlic
2 tablespoons polyunsaturated oil
1 cup chicken stock or water
125 g (4 oz) walnuts
2 teaspoons cornflour

METHOD

1. Dice chicken and stem mushrooms or soak dried mushrooms in boiling water until soft
2. Cut mushrooms into strips
3. Mix chicken with soy and brandy or dry sherry and salt
4. Place oil in a pan with garlic and heat till garlic is brown
5. Add chicken to pan and stir briskly
6. When chicken is almost cooked add celery and mushrooms
7. Stir well for 5–10 minutes, add walnuts
8. Finally add water which has been blended with cornflour; allow to boil

Per serve: 1½ tablespoons oil equivalent   Serves 4

CHICKEN IN THE BASKET

*Four small chickens 0.5–0.7 kg (1–1½ lb) in weight
or two 1.0–1.1 kg (2–2½ lb) chickens
Salt, pepper
Polyunsaturated margarine
2 teaspoons paprika
Water or stock*

METHOD

1. Truss chickens, rub with salt and pepper
2. Spread breasts and thighs with margarine, place on rack in baking dish; sprinkle with paprika
3. Pour in approximately 1 cup stock or water
4. Bake in moderately hot oven 1–¼ hours or until chickens are well browned and tender; baste frequently
5. Add extra water to pan during cooking if necessary
6. To serve, place chickens in small individual baskets lined with paper napkins   Serves 4

CHICKEN RIOJANA

*1 chicken 1.0–1.1 kg (2–2½ lb)
Salt and pepper to taste
Seasoned flour
100 ml (3 fl oz) polyunsaturated oil
1 clove crushed garlic
3 shallots chopped or ¼ cup chopped onion
¼ cup chopped red pepper
½ cup drained whole kernel corn
1½ cups cooked long grain rice
¾ cup finely chopped small onions
1 cup apricot nectar
1 tablespoon white vinegar or
2 tablespoons white wine
3 peeled chopped tomatoes*

METHOD

1. Cut chicken into serving pieces, coat with seasoned flour
2. Pour sufficient oil to cover base of large frying pan. Add chicken and fry, turning for even browning

3. Reduce heat, cover and cook until tender, about 30–40 minutes
4. Serve on a bed of Rice Riojana or hot boiled rice and spoon Riojana sauce over chicken pieces

RICE RIOJANA

1. Heat 30 ml (1 fl oz) oil
2. Add garlic, white part of shallots or onion and red pepper; cook 3 minutes
3. Add corn and rice and toss well with fork, cooking until heated
4. Add salt and pepper to taste and serve sprinkled with green shallots

RIOJANA SAUCE

1. Heat 30 ml (1 fl oz) oil, add onions, cook slowly until tender; do not brown
2. Add apricot nectar and wine, bring to the boil and continue boiling fast to reduce liquid and thicken
3. Add salt and pepper to taste
4. Add tomatoes, simmer gently to heat

Per serve: 30 ml (1 fl oz) oil   Serves 4

CREAMED CHICKEN

*1.0–1.1 kg (2–2½ lb) steamed chicken carved
into serving portions
3 cups coating white sauce (p. 83)
1 cup cooked peas
2 cups fried crumbs (p. 90)*

METHOD

1. Combine chicken, white sauce and peas
2. Place in casserole dish, sprinkle with fried crumbs and heat in moderate oven

Per serve: 75 ml (2½ fl oz) oil minimum   Serves 4

CURRIED TURKEY

*100 ml (3 fl oz) polyunsaturated oil
1 cup diced onion
2 cups diced cooking apple*

Salt and pepper
2 teaspoons curry powder
2 tablespoons flour
2 cups skim milk with 2 chicken cubes added
1 tablespoon lemon juice
4 cups cooked diced turkey

METHOD

1. Heat ¼ cup oil, add onion and apple and cook until tender, about 15 minutes
2. Remove mixture from pan, add remaining oil and blend in salt, pepper, curry powder and flour
3. Return to heat and cook 1 minute. Remove from heat, add liquid and lemon juice and reheat, stirring constantly until mixture thickens
4. Add meat, apple and onions and allow to simmer for 15 minutes

Per serve: 1½ tablespoons oil   Serves 4

HAWAIIAN RICE

100 ml (3 fl oz) polyunsaturated oil
1 cup uncooked rice
2 cups chicken stock
Salt and pepper to taste
1 cup chopped onion
1 cup chopped green or red pepper
½ cup chopped celery
1–2 teaspoons curry powder
425 g (15 oz) can pineapple pieces
2 cups chopped cooked chicken

METHOD

1. Heat half the oil in frying pan, add rice and brown lightly
2. Reduce heat, add stock and seasonings. Cook gently with lid on for about 20 minutes or until rice is tender
3. In large saucepan heat remainder in the oil, add onion, pepper, celery, curry powder and cook gently until tender
4. Add vegetables, drained pineapple pieces and chicken pieces to rice mixture
5. Stir ingredients through and heat thoroughly

Per serve: 1½ tablespoons oil   Serves 4

Fried rice: Omit pineapple pieces, curry powder and chicken
Flavour with soy sauce

RABBIT CASSEROLE
1 rabbit
Salt and pepper to taste
Pinch nutmeg
1 small pkt asparagus soup reconstituted
1 cup skim milk
2 heaped tablespoons flour
Fried breadcrumbs (p. 90)

METHOD
1. Steam rabbit until meat leaves the bones
2. Chop coarsely and season with salt, pepper and a pinch of nutmeg
3. In a saucepan place the soup and milk and stir in flour which has been mixed with a little cold water
4. Stir until it thickens; add chopped rabbit
5. Arrange in large casserole dish, sprinkle with fried breadcrumbs and bake in moderate oven for 30 minutes

Per serve: 2 teaspoons oil   Serves 4

RABBIT IN CIDER
1 rabbit or 4 quarters
Juice of half lemon
½ cup polyunsaturated oil
4 cups diced onions
1 bay leaf
Thyme
375 g (¾ lb) peeled and sliced tomatoes
Salt and pepper
⅔ cup dry cider

METHOD
1. Joint rabbit into 4 pieces, soak in lukewarm water to which lemon juice has been added; remove pieces from water and dry well
2. Heat oil in pan and brown pieces of rabbit; add diced onion

3. When onions are soft add bay leaf and a little thyme
4. Cook for about 10 minutes then add sliced tomatoes and simmer for a further 10 minutes
5. Pour in dry cider, let liquid bubble fiercely for a minute or so, reduce heat and simmer with lid on until rabbit is tender
6. Add a little seasoning if necessary and remove bay leaf

Per serve: 30 ml (1 fl oz) oil   Serves 4

WHOLE CHICKEN BRAISED WITH MUSHROOMS

1.0–1.1 kg (2–2½ lb) chicken
Salt
60 g (2 oz) dried mushrooms or
6–8 fresh mushrooms
3 cloves garlic
2 teaspoons soy sauce
1 tablespoon brandy or dry sherry
3 tablespoons polyunsaturated oil

METHOD

1. Salt chicken thoroughly
2. Scald and stem the dried mushrooms
3. Crush two cloves garlic and mix well with soy sauce and brandy then rub the mixture all over the chicken
4. Add one clove garlic to oil and heat in a large saucepan until garlic browns
5. Place chicken in saucepan and allow to brown well; add mushrooms
6. Stir well, then add 2½ cups water and balance of mixture (soy, brandy, etc.)
7. Bring to boil and allow to simmer for approximately 1 hour
8. If required, cornflour blended with water may be used to thicken gravy

Per serve: 3 teaspoons oil   Serves 4

RABBIT IN RED WINE

1 rabbit or 4 quarters
3 tablespoons polyunsaturated oil
2½ cups finely chopped onions
1 cup diced potatoes

1 clove crushed garlic
Salt
1 tablespoon dry breadcrumbs
Black pepper
1¼ cups red wine

METHOD

1. Divide rabbit into pieces
2. Heat oil in shallow pan
3. Wipe pieces of rabbit and sauté until they are golden brown on all sides
4. Remove rabbit from pan, sauté the onions and potatoes in remaining fat and add the crushed garlic
5. When onions begin to brown return rabbit to pan, season with salt, lower heat and add dry breadcrumbs with ground pepper. Pour in the red wine; taste for seasoning and put the dish uncovered in a moderate oven for about 20 minutes

Per serve: 1 tablespoon oil   Serves 4

VARIATIONS

Chicken or duck could replace rabbit in this dish

VEGETABLES

Vegetables contain no cholesterol and the small content of fat is generally polyunsaturated fat. There is therefore no restriction on either the variety or quantity that may be eaten. Vegetables, moreover, form good vehicles for increasing the amount of polyunsaturated oils and margarine which may be consumed each day.

Polyunsaturated oil may be used when baking, deep or shallow frying, sautéing and mashing vegetables.

Polyunsaturated margarine may be used with steamed vegetables.

Parsley, garlic and herb spreads (p. 90) may also be used as garnishes for vegetables.

Polyunsaturated margarine and oil may be used when making the white sauces (p. 82) or your own favourite sauces to serve with vegetables.

GLAZED CARROTS

¼ cup chopped onion
60 g (2 oz) polyunsaturated margarine
2 cups thinly sliced carrots
⅓ cup water
Salt and pepper to taste
½ teaspoon brown sugar

METHOD

1. Sauté onions in margarine until golden
2. Add carrots and cook a few more minutes
3. Add water, pepper, salt and sugar
4. Cover and simmer over low heat until tender

Per serve: 1½ teaspoons oil equivalent   Serves 4

VARIATION

Substitute: peas, parsnip, potato, sweet potato, sweet corn, red cabbage

MASHED POTATOES

2 cups cooked potato
60 g (2 oz) polyunsaturated margarine or
1 tablespoon polyunsaturated oil

METHOD

1. Mash potatoes, add margarine or oil and beat until light and fluffy

Per serve: 1 teaspoon oil minimum   Serves 4

SAFFRON RICE

2½ cups chicken stock
¼ teaspoon saffron
3 tablespoons polyunsaturated oil
¾ cup chopped onion
1 clove chopped garlic
½ cup chopped green pepper
250 g (½ lb) rice

METHOD

1. Infuse the saffron, whether ground or whole, in the chicken stock
2. Heat oil in fireproof casserole. Add onion, garlic, pepper and rice. Turn rice until grains are well coated with oil
3. Add saffron-flavoured chicken stock
4. Bring to boil, cover and bake in a moderate oven for 30 minutes

Per serve: 1 tablespoon oil   Serves 4

SAUTÉ FRENCH BEANS

1¼ cups sliced french beans
90 g (3 oz) polyunsaturated margarine
3 tablespoons water
Salt, pepper
Squeeze of lemon juice
Chopped parsley

METHOD

1. Cook beans in margarine, water, salt, pepper and lemon juice until tender. Add parsley

Per serve: 3 teaspoons oil equivalent   Serves 4

VARIATION

Substitute onions, carrots, marrow, tomatoes or finely shredded cabbage for french beans

SCALLOPED POTATOES

500 g (1 lb) potatoes
Pepper and salt
1 tablespoon flour
2 tablespoons polyunsaturated margarine
1¼ cups skim milk

METHOD

1. Peel potatoes and cut into thin slices
2. Arrange in layers in greased pie dish with a little pepper, salt and flour between each layer

3. Pour in the milk and add dots of margarine
4. Place in moderate oven for 40–45 minutes

Per serve: 1 teaspoon oil   Serves 4

STUFFED GREEN PEPPERS

4 large green peppers
1¼ cups thick white sauce (p. 83)
1½ cups diced cold cooked meat
1 cup whole kernel corn
½ teaspoon mustard
1 cup fried breadcrumbs (p. 90)

METHOD

1. Cut stem ends from peppers and remove seed. Chop ends
2. Place cases into boiling salted water, simmer for 5 minutes then remove
3. Cook chopped pepper ends for about 2 minutes in salted water, then drain
4. Prepare the sauce, add cold cooked meat, corn, mustard and chopped pepper ends
5. Fill pepper cases – they can be placed into deep patty tins to hold them upright
6. Sprinkle fried breadcrumbs on top of pepper
7. Bake in a moderately hot oven until pepper is tender, approximately 15 minutes

Per serve: 5½ teaspoons oil equivalent   Serves 4

TOMATO SCALLOP

1 tablespoon polyunsaturated margarine
½ cup breadcrumbs
4 sliced tomatoes
2 thinly sliced cooking apples
1 cup thinly sliced onion rings
Salt and pepper
2 cups fried crumbs (p. 90)

METHOD

1. Grease the bottom and sides of an ovenproof dish with margarine and sprinkle with breadcrumbs

2. Fill the dish with layers of sliced tomato, apple, and thinly sliced onion rings; season with salt and pepper
3. Cover with fried crumbs and bake at least one hour in a slow oven

Per serve: 30 ml (1 fl oz) oil Serves 4

VEGETABLE SAUTÉ WITH TARRAGON DRESSING

2 cups beans cut into 5 cm (2 inch) diagonal slices
2 cups sliced courgette
1 cup carrot rings
500 g (1 lb) small white onions sliced
Salt
3 tablespoons polyunsaturated oil
2 tablespoons polyunsaturated margarine
¼ teaspoon Tabasco sauce
Tarragon dressing (p. 82)

METHOD

1. Cook vegetables in boiling salted water until they are tender but still crisp; drain
2. Heat oil and margarine in pan. Stir in Tabasco sauce
3. Add all vegetables and toss gently until heated through, about 5 minutes
4. Serve immediately with tarragon dressing

Per serve: 3 teaspoons oil minimum   Serves 4

SALADS

There are no restrictions on either the quantity or variety of vegetables which may be used for salads. Therefore the increased use of salads either as the main course or as a side dish with a grill, fish or poultry is encouraged because the accompanying salad dressing can be made with oils containing polyunsaturated fats.

Polyunsaturated mayonnaise or boiled dressing (p. 80) may also be used as the binding agent in potato, rice, macaroni or mixed vegetable salads.

Safflower, sunflower, soybean and corn oils are recommended as the base for salad dressings because of their high content of polyunsaturated fats. Olive oil and peanut oil have a low polyunsaturated fat content and are not recommended as a base.

Cottage cheese and cottage cheese dips (p. 88) as a substitute for meat are useful additions to salads.

CABBAGE SALAD

2 cups finely shredded green cabbage
1 tablespoon finely chopped onion
2 tablespoons finely chopped celery
Salt and pepper to taste
¾ cup cottage cheese
Polyunsaturated mayonnaise

METHOD
1. Combine cabbage, onion, celery, salt and pepper
2. Fold cottage cheese lightly through mixture
3. Add sufficient mayonnaise to moisten   Serves 4

COTTAGE CHEESE POTATO SALAD

2 cups cooked diced potatoes
¼ cup sliced celery
1 tablespoon chopped green pepper
2 teaspoons chopped pimento
1 tablespoon grated onion
1 tablespoon chopped pickles
½ cup polyunsaturated mayonnaise
½ teaspoon salt
½ teaspoon dry mustard
Pinch pepper
2 teaspoons lemon juice
½ cup cottage cheese

METHOD
1. Combine potatoes, celery, green pepper, pimento, onion and pickles. Chill well
2. Blend mayonnaise, salt, pepper, mustard and lemon juice
3. Pour over potato mixture and add cottage cheese. Toss lightly

Per serve: 3 teaspoons oil equivalent   Serves 4

ITALIAN SALAD

¾ cup cooked diced carrots
¾ cup asparagus cuts
¾ cup cooked peas
1 tablespoon chopped parsley
Polyunsaturated mayonnaise

METHOD

1. Bind vegetables with mayonnaise   Serves 4

May also be served as cocktail by placing on a bed of shredded lettuce in a cocktail glass

MARINADED CUCUMBER

1 peeled cucumber, 250 g (8 oz)
½ cup french dressing (p. 80)

METHOD

1. Slice cucumber paper thin
2. Cover with dressing

Per serve: 30 ml (1 fl oz) oil   Serves 4

MARINADED GREEN BEANS

1½ cups finely cut beans
2 tablespoons chopped onions
½ teaspoon coarse ground pepper
4 tablespoons vinegar
3 tablespoons polyunsaturated oil
Pinch of basil

METHOD

1. Cook beans in boiling salted water 4–5 minutes. Drain well
2. Mix beans with rest of ingredients, cover and chill well

Per serve: 1 tablespoon oil   Serves 4

RAISIN SALAD

½ cup raisins
1 cup grated carrot
¼ cup finely diced onion
¾ cup diced celery
¼ small cabbage, finely shredded
Salt and pepper
Polyunsaturated mayonnaise

METHOD

1. Mix all ingredients together, season to taste with salt and pepper
2. Add sufficient mayonnaise to bind ingredients

Serves 4

RICE SALAD

2 cups cooked rice
(approximately ¾ cup uncooked)
3 tablespoons polyunsaturated mayonnaise
½ cup cooked peas
½ cup diced carrots
½ cup diced red apple
1 cup finely sliced celery
2 teaspoons salt
¼ teaspoon pepper

METHOD

1. Combine all ingredients

Per serve: 3 teaspoons oil equivalent   Serves 4

WALDORF SALAD

2 cups diced unpeeled red apples
2 tablespoons lemon juice
1 cup chopped celery
½ cup polyunsaturated mayonnaise
½ cup coarsely chopped walnuts

METHOD

1. Sprinkle apples with lemon juice, mix with celery, bind with mayonnaise. Chill
2. Just before serving add chopped walnuts

Per serve: 6 teaspoons oil equivalent   Serves 4

2½ cups yoghurt
1 teaspoon caraway seeds
1½ teaspoons curry powder
1 tablespoon chopped onion
1½ teaspoons garlic salt
2 cups cold diced potatoes

METHOD

1. Combine yoghurt, caraway seeds, curry powder, onion and garlic salt
2. Fold mixture into diced potato; chill a few hours before serving

Serves 4

CAKES AND BISCUITS

Favourite family recipes can be adapted to suit this Modified Fat Diet by substituting skim milk for full cream milk and polyunsaturated margarine for butter or other margarines.

Egg yolks used in cakes and biscuits must be counted as part of the total allowance of three per person per week. This restriction does not apply to egg whites as these do not contain cholesterol.

Commercially prepared cakes and biscuits should only be used occasionally as the quantity and type of fat and the number of eggs used in their preparation are unknown. Biscuits with cream fillings and those with chocolate coatings should not be eaten.

Use packet cakes no more than once a week because although you can control the use of eggs and skim milk in the preparation, the type and quantity of fat in the mixture is unknown.

Use polyunsaturated margarine or oil for greasing tins or paper in preparation for cooking.

Do not use cream as a filling or for decoration. Mock cream (p. 68) is a good substitution.

APPLE CAKE

125 g (4 oz) polyunsaturated margarine
125 g (4 oz) castor sugar
1 tablespoon chopped lemon peel
1 teaspoon cinnamon
½ teaspoon spice
1 cup drained stewed apples
2 cups S.R. flour

METHOD

1. Cream margarine with sugar; add lemon peel
2. Fold in apples, then sifted flour and spices and mix lightly but thoroughly
3. Pour into well-greased 20 cm (8 inch) round tin
4. Sprinkle top with cinnamon crumble topping (p. 73)
5. Bake in moderate oven for 20–25 minutes
6. Warm icing (p. 69) and chopped walnuts may be used instead of cinnamon crumble topping

CHOCOLATE CAKE

125 g (4 oz) polyunsaturated margarine
125 g (4 oz) castor sugar
Vanilla essence
2 tablespoons golden syrup
2½ cups plain flour
4 tablespoons cocoa
4 teaspoons baking powder
1 teaspoon bicarbonate of soda
1½ cups skim milk

METHOD

1. Cream margarine with sugar, vanilla and syrup
2. Fold in sifted dry ingredients alternately with milk making a soft dropping consistency
3. Grease and line bottoms of two 20 cm (8 inch) sandwich tins; fill mixture evenly into both
4. Bake in moderate oven for 30–35 minutes
5. Cool on cake cooler, fill with lemon filling, dust top with sifted icing sugar or decorate with warm icing (p. 69) and chopped walnuts

Lemon filling

Grated rind and juice of one lemon
3 teaspoons cornflour
3 tablespoons water
4 tablespoons sugar
3 teaspoons polyunsaturated margarine

METHOD

1. Blend cornflour with water
2. Place all ingredients in saucepan, stir constantly over gentle heat until boiling. Simmer 3 minutes
3. Allow to cool then spread evenly between cakes

CHRISTMAS CAKE

2 cups water
1¾ cups sugar
2 tablespoons golden syrup
125 g (4 oz) polyunsaturated margarine
3 cups sultanas, currants and chopped raisins
60 g (2 oz) each glacé pineapple, apricots, cherries and dried figs
2 tablespoons chopped peel
30 g (1 oz) glacé pears
¼ cup chopped walnuts
3 tablespoons sherry or whisky
3 cups plain flour
1 cup S.R. flour
1 teaspoon bicarbonate soda
1 teaspoon each spice, cinnamon, nutmeg
¼ teaspoon salt
1 teaspoon each vanilla, lemon essence
3 drops almond essence

METHOD

1. Soak mixed fruit in sherry overnight
2. Place water, sugar, syrup, margarine and fruit into a saucepan and bring to boil. Boil for 10 minutes, cool
3. Add sifted dry ingredients and vanilla, lemon and almond essence
4. Pour into a well-lined 20 cm (8 inch) round or square tin and bake in very moderate oven for 1¼–1½ hours

FRUIT NUT LOAF

½ cup sultanas
1 cup water
60 g (2 oz) castor sugar
60 g (2 oz) polyunsaturated margarine
1 teaspoon soda
1 egg
1 teaspoon cinnamon
½ cup chopped walnuts
2 cups S.R. flour
Pinch salt

METHOD

1. Place sultanas, water, sugar, margarine and soda into a saucepan, bring to the boil, simmer three minutes, then allow to cool
2. Add beaten egg, cinnamon and walnuts
3. Fold in sifted flour and salt
4. Pour into greased loaf tin and bake in moderate oven 35–40 minutes
5. Serve cold cut into slices and spread with polyunsaturated margarine

GINGERBREAD

1 teaspoon bicarbonate soda
1 cup skim milk
2 teaspoons ground ginger
1 teaspoon cinnamon
1 teaspoon mixed spice
2 cups plain flour
125 g (4 oz) polyunsaturated margarine
60 g (2 oz) castor sugar
1 cup warm golden syrup
¼ cup walnuts
1 cup mixed fruit – including peel

METHOD

1. Dissolve the soda in the milk. Add spices to sifted flour
2. Cream margarine and sugar thoroughly and beat in the warm golden syrup
3. Fold milk and flour alternately into creamed mixture

4. Add walnuts and mixed fruit
5. Bake in 20 cm (8 inch) square tin in slow to moderate oven, approximately 30 minutes
6. Either ice with lemon icing when cold and decorate with pieces of candied ginger or lemon peel or spread slices with polyunsaturated margarine

ORANGE AND RAISIN SLICE

125 g (4 oz) polyunsaturated margarine
1 cup brown sugar
1 egg
1 cup sifted plain flour
½ teaspoon soda
1 teaspoon baking powder
¼ teaspoon salt
1 cup buttermilk
Rind and juice of 1 small orange
1 cup raisins
1 cup uncooked rolled oats

METHOD
1. Cream margarine; gradually add sugar, creaming thoroughly
2. Add egg and beat until light and fluffy
3. Sift together flour, soda, baking powder and salt. Add to creamed mixture alternately with buttermilk
4. Finely chop raisins, mix with orange juice and rind. Fold mixture into batter
5. Add rolled oats, mixing lightly until combined
6. Bake in a greased 18 × 28 cm (7 × 11 inch) tin in a moderate oven for 45 to 50 minutes

May be served as a hot dessert with hard sauce (p. 74) or custard (p. 74)

ORANGE BISCUITS

⅔ cup brown sugar
3 tablespoons polyunsaturated oil
1 egg white
1 teaspoon grated orange rind
3 tablespoons orange juice

1½ cups sifted flour
½ teaspoon soda
½ teaspoon baking powder
Chopped walnuts

METHOD

1. Mix brown sugar with oil, beat in egg white, add orange juice and grated orange rind
2. Sift flour with soda and baking powder and stir into mixture
3. Drop with teaspoon on to tray and bake about 8–10 minutes in moderate oven
4. When biscuits are cool, ice with orange icing (p. 69) and decorate with walnuts

PLAIN SCONES

2 cups S.R. flour
1 tablespoon icing sugar
2 tablespoons polyunsaturated margarine
About ¾ cup skim milk

METHOD

1. Combine sifted flour with sugar
2. Melt margarine, add to milk
3. Pour liquid all at once into dry ingredients
4. Mix quickly into soft dough
5. Turn on to floured board and knead lightly and quickly
6. Roll out to 1.5 cm (about ½–¾ inch) thick and cut into desired shape. Place on lightly greased tray. Glaze with milk
7. Cook in hot oven for 10–12 minutes

VARIATIONS

Add to above mixture

Spicy fruit scones: 1 teaspoon mixed spices, ¼ cup chopped mixed fruit
Sultana scones: ½ cup chopped sultanas
Date scones: ¼ cup chopped dates
Currant scones: ¼ cup currants
Walnut scones: ¼ cup chopped walnuts
Orange scones: grated rind and juice of 1 orange. Reduce

quantities of milk so that total liquid used equals $\frac{3}{4}$ cup. Brush with orange juice and sprinkle with sugar before baking

WALNUT CRESCENTS

Pastry:
125 g (4 oz) cottage cheese
125 g (4 oz) polyunsaturated margarine
1 cup plain flour

METHOD

1. Mix ingredients and knead thoroughly. Cover and let stand 2–12 hours
2. Roll pastry thinly and bake in moderately hot oven after filling with various fillings

Walnut filling:
1 cup walnut pieces
⅓ cup hot skim milk
6 tablespoons sugar

The following are optional but improve the flavour:

Grated lemon peel
Cinnamon
1 tablespoon honey
2 tablespoons sultanas

METHOD

1. Grind walnuts finely, pour boiling milk over them
2. Add rest of ingredients. If walnuts are old and have strong flavour add 1 tablespoon breadcrumbs and a little more milk
3. Roll pastry out thinly. Cut into squares about 8 × 8 cm (3 × 3 inches). Place walnut mixture in centre, fold a corner of a square in about halfway so that folded corner will cover the filling, then roll the triangle and bend it in the shape of a crescent
4. Bake in moderately hot oven
5. When cool dust with icing sugar

VARIATIONS

Jam triangles

1. Roll out pastry, cut into 5 × 5 cm (2 × 2 inch) or 8 × 8 cm (3 × 3 inch) squares, add jam

2. Fold in half diagonally, pressing down edges
3. Bake as above. When cool dust with icing sugar

Apple strudel

Filling:
1 cup hot fried crumbs (p. 90)
4 coarsely grated or thinly sliced large apples
3 tablespoons sultanas
3 tablespoons sugar
1 teaspoon cinnamon
Grated rind of 1 lemon
Pinch powdered cloves

METHOD

1. Roll out pastry into large rectangle
2. Fill centre with apple, sprinkle with remaining ingredients. Leave outer edges of pastry free of filling
3. Fold pastry in from the sides to overlap in the centre and slightly fold in the ends so that filling is completely enclosed
4. Bake as above. When cool dust with icing sugar

MOCK CREAM

2 tablespoons polyunsaturated margarine
2 tablespoons sugar
1 tablespoon boiling water
1 tablespoon cold skim milk
Vanilla essence

METHOD

1. Beat margarine and sugar until light and fluffy
2. Gradually add boiling water then milk, beating well
3. Flavour with vanilla
4. Use with desserts and as fillings for cakes, biscuits etc.

VIENNA MOCK CREAM

2 tablespoons polyunsaturated margarine
1 teaspoon vanilla essence
8 tablespoons sifted icing sugar
1 tablespoon skim milk

1. Combine all ingredients
2. Whip until light and fluffy
3. Use as a filling or force through an icing tube to decorate cakes or tarts, coloured and flavoured as desired

WARM ICING

1 cup icing sugar
1 tablespoon polyunsaturated margarine (melted)
Water

METHOD

1. Sift icing sugar and mix with melted margarine and a little water until icing is smooth and thick
2. Warm slightly over low heat
3. Use as required

VARIATIONS

Coffee: Add 1 teaspoon instant coffee powder to icing sugar
Chocolate: Add 1 tablespoon cocoa to icing sugar
Lemon: Use strained lemon juice instead of water
Orange: Use strained orange juice instead of water

DESSERTS

Favourite recipes can be adapted to meet this Modified Fat Diet by substituting skim milk for full cream milk, and polyunsaturated margarine for butter or other margarines.

Egg yolks used in desserts must be counted as part of the total allowance of three per person per week. This restriction does not apply to egg whites as these do not contain cholesterol.

Packet and commercially prepared pastries, puddings, etc. should only be used occasionally as the quantity and type of fat which these products contain are unknown.

Commercially prepared ice creams and milk ices contain

saturated fats and these products must therefore be eaten only occasionally. Water ices can be freely used.

Cream must not be used either as an ingredient when making the dessert or for decoration. Mock cream (p. 68) or hard sauce (p. 74) could be used as substitutes for decoration.

Desserts which do not require egg yolk, butter, cream or full cream milk are *unrestricted*.

Use polyunsaturated margarine or oil for greasing tins, ovenproof dishes and paper in preparation for cooking desserts.

BAKED APPLE ROLL

1 cup S.R. flour
1 teaspoon cinnamon
75 g (2½ oz) polyunsaturated margarine
3 tablespoons water
1½ cups cooked apples (sweetened to taste)
½ cup sultanas
½ cup chopped walnuts
¼ cup brown sugar
½ cup boiling water

METHOD

1. Sift flour, cinnamon into bowl
2. Rub in 60 g (2 oz) margarine until mixture resembles breadcrumbs
3. Mix to firm dough with water
4. Turn on to floured board and roll to an oblong shape 1 cm (¼ inch) thick
5. Mix cooked apples, sultanas, walnuts together
6. Cover the roll with apple mixture leaving 2.5 cm (1 inch) margin all round
7. Roll up, close ends and place in pie dish
8. Dissolve brown sugar and 15 g (½ oz) margarine in boiling water and pour this round the roll
9. Bake in hot oven 20 minutes and then reduce to moderate oven. Bake until cooked through, 30–35 minutes
10. Serve warm with custard (p. 74)

Per serve: 4 teaspoons oil   Serves 4

4 bananas
Lemon juice
½ cup castor sugar
1 teaspoon cinnamon
Polyunsaturated margarine
100 ml (3 fl oz) warmed brandy

METHOD

1. Peel and halve bananas, place in shallow fireproof dish and sprinkle with lemon juice
2. Combine sugar and cinnamon and sprinkle over top of bananas
3. Dot liberally with margarine
4. Place under medium hot grill until soft and golden
5. Take to table, pour over brandy and ignite

Serves 4

CHEESE CAKE

Base:
90 g (3 oz) polyunsaturated margarine
60 g (2 oz) icing sugar
1 cup S.R. flour
2 tablespoons skim milk

METHOD

1. Sift flour and icing sugar into bowl. Rub in margarine
2. Add skim milk and mix until mixture forms a ball
3. Spread over base of greased spring form tin
4. Bake in a moderate oven for 10–15 minutes

Filling:
2 teaspoons gelatine
Pinch salt
1 egg
½ cup skim milk
375 g (12 oz) cottage cheese
3 tablespoons dried skim milk powder
Vanilla essence
6 tablespoons castor sugar
Rind and juice 1 large lemon

METHOD

1. Mix together gelatine and salt
2. Separate egg, beat yolk with skim milk
3. Add gelatine mixture, stir over low heat until gelatine dissolves
4. Remove from heat, add lemon rind, cool
5. Sieve cheese, beat in dried skim milk powder, gelatine mixture, lemon juice, vanilla and 4 tablespoons sugar
6. Beat egg white until stiff, gradually add remainder of sugar and beat well
7. Fold into cheese mixture
8. Spoon on to prepared base and refrigerate until firm

Per serve: 1 teaspoon oil equivalent   Serves 12

CHOCOLATE SAUCE PUDDING

1 cup S.R. flour
1 tablespoon cocoa
$\frac{3}{4}$ cup castor sugar
90 g (3 oz) polyunsaturated margarine
$\frac{1}{2}$ cup skim milk
1 teaspoon vanilla essence
2 cups hot water

Topping:
$\frac{3}{4}$ cup brown sugar and 1 tablespoon cocoa

METHOD

1. Sift together flour and cocoa, add castor sugar
2. Heat margarine and milk in saucepan, add vanilla
3. Fold into flour mixture until smooth
4. Pour into deep greased ovenproof dish
5. Combine topping ingredients, sprinkle on top of pudding. Gently pour over hot water
6. Bake in moderate oven for 40–45 minutes

N.B. 1 tablespoon of chopped walnuts may be added to the batter

Per serve: 3 teaspoons oil equivalent   Serves 4

CHRISTMAS PUDDING

140 g (4½ oz) polyunsaturated margarine
1½ cups plain flour
3 cups soft white breadcrumbs
1½ cups brown sugar
1½ cups chopped sultanas
1½ cups chopped raisins
¾ cup currants
60 g (2 oz) grated carrot
60 g (2 oz) chopped peel
½ cup chopped walnuts
3 level teaspoons bicarbonate soda
1½ cups skim milk
(or 1 cup skim milk + ½ cup brandy)

METHOD

1. Rub margarine into flour, add breadcrumbs, brown sugar and prepared fruits, nuts and carrot
2. Dissolve bicarbonate of soda in milk and add to dry ingredients.
3. Grease a 2.5 l (4 pint) size pudding basin and ¾ fill with mixture
4. Tie on muslin pudding cloth and place into saucepan of boiling water. Steam 3 hours
5. Store in cool dry place. If storing in deep freeze turn on to a plate and wrap in plastic
6. When required steam 2 hours   Serves 12

CINNAMON CRUMBLE TOPPING

¼ cup brown sugar
125 g (4 oz) melted polyunsaturated margarine
¾ cup flour
¾ cup crushed cornflake crumbs
2 teaspoons cinnamon

METHOD

1. Cream sugar and melted margarine and mix in other ingredients
2. Sprinkle over top of cakes or stewed fruit before placing into the oven

CREAMED RICE

60 g (2 oz) polyunsaturated margarine
3 tablespoons rice
½ cup water
2½ cups skim milk
2 tablespoons sugar

METHOD

1. Grease ovenproof dish with a little margarine
2. Put rice and water in dish and cook in slow oven until rice absorbs water, stirring occasionally
3. Melt 30 g (1 oz) margarine gently and whisk into skim milk and sugar
4. Add to rice, sprinkle with nutmeg and bake in a slow oven for 1–1½ hours

Per serve: 2 teaspoons oil equivalent   Serves 4

CUSTARD

2 tablespoons custard powder
2½ cups skim milk
2 tablespoons sugar
½ cup polyunsaturated oil
Vanilla essence

METHOD

1. Blend custard powder with a little milk until smooth and free from lumps
2. Place remaining milk and sugar into saucepan and heat till not quite boiling
3. Remove from hotplate, stir in blended custard powder and return to heat
4. Stir continuously until mixture boils and thickens; add vanilla
5. Remove from heat and beat in the oil gradually

Per serve: 30 ml (1 fl oz) oil   Serves 4

HARD SAUCE

125 g (4 oz) polyunsaturated margarine
185 g (6 oz) icing sugar
⅓ cup brandy or sherry

1. Cream margarine and icing sugar until light and fluffy
2. Gradually beat in brandy or sherry

ICE CREAM

2½ cups water
2 cups dried skim milk powder
3 tablespoons sugar
2 teaspoons gelatine dissolved in 2 tablespoons
boiling water
60 g (2 oz) polyunsaturated margarine
Flavouring

METHOD

1. Warm water, add powdered milk and sugar and beat well
2. Add the dissolved gelatine, melted margarine and beat for 5 minutes
3. Turn refrigerator to maximum. Quick freezing makes a smoother ice cream. Pour mixture into refrigerator trays and chill
4. When ice cream is firm but not hard (approximately ¾ hour) remove from trays and beat ice cream until double its volume. Do this as quickly as possible. Add flavouring
5. Pour into two trays, return to refrigerator and when firm turn control to normal setting

FLAVOURINGS

Vanilla ice cream: 2 teaspoons vanilla essence
Orange ice cream: 2 teaspoons grated orange rind
Coffee ice cream: 1 tablespoon instant coffee powder blended with a little hot water and added to mixture
Chocolate ice cream: 45 g (1½ oz) cocoa blended with a little hot water and added to mixture
Strawberry ice cream: ½ cup crushed strawberries
Banana ice cream: ¾ cup mashed bananas sprinkled with lemon juice
Pineapple ice cream: ¾ cup drained crushed pineapple substituting 2 tablespoons pineapple syrup for water

Mocha and walnut ice cream: 2 teaspoons instant coffee powder and 30 g (1 oz) cocoa blended with a little hot water and $\frac{1}{4}$ cup chopped walnuts

JUNKET

1½ tablespoons sugar
2½ cups skim milk
2 junket tablets
2 teaspoons vanilla essence

METHOD

1. Add sugar to milk and warm to blood heat
2. Crush junket tablets and dissolve in a little water
3. Add crushed junket tablets and vanilla to skim milk and pour into dish, sprinkle with nutmeg
4. Stand aside to set   Serves 4

VARIATIONS

Coffee: Add 1 tablespoon powdered instant coffee to skim milk
Coloured: Few drops of colouring
Chocolate: Mix 1 level tablespoon cocoa and 1 tablespoon boiling water and add to milk

LEMON MERINGUE PIE

1 quantity of sweet pastry (p. 78)
6 tablespoons sugar
½ cup lemon juice
Grated rind 1 lemon
1 cup water
5½ tablespoons cornflour
125 g (4 oz) polyunsaturated margarine
2 egg whites
4 tablespoons castor sugar

METHOD

1. Roll pastry out to fit 20 cm (8 inch) pie plate, prick well and bake in moderate oven for 10–15 minutes
2. Combine sugar, lemon juice, lemon rind, water and

cornflour and blend well. Boil for three minutes, stirring continually
3. Add margarine and beat well
4. Allow to cool then pour into cooked pie shell
5. Beat egg whites until stiff, gradually add castor sugar and beat well
6. Spoon on top of lemon filling. Return pie to oven until meringue has browned

Per serve: 1½ tablespoons oil   Serves 6

PANCAKES

1 cup S.R. flour
Pinch salt
2½ cups skim milk
2 egg whites
1 tablespoon polyunsaturated oil
Margarine (polyunsaturated) for cooking

METHOD
1. Sift flour and salt into a bowl
2. Make a well in centre, add milk, gradually mixing well all the time. When all milk is added the mixture should be smooth and thin
3. Beat egg whites until just stiff and fold evenly through the batter
4. Stir in the oil
5. Pour mixture into a jug
6. Heat a little margarine in frying pan until well browned
7. Wipe this out and melt a little more margarine
8. When this is just bubbling, pour in sufficient batter to make thin pancakes the size you desire. Pancakes may be used as dessert or as a savoury dish when filled with meat or fish filling, i.e. Mexican rice (p. 39); savoury meat sauce (p. 112); salmon wizz (p. 33)

Makes 9–12 pancakes

VARIATION
Pikelets
Reduce quantity of skim milk to half
Method as above

QUICK BANANA DESSERT

4 bananas
Lemon juice
100 ml (3 fl oz) orange juice
½ cup castor sugar
1 teaspoon cinnamon
¼ cup chopped walnuts
Polyunsaturated margarine

METHOD

1. Peel and halve bananas, place in a shallow ovenproof dish and sprinkle with lemon juice
2. Pour in orange juice
3. Combine sugar, cinnamon and walnuts and sprinkle over top of bananas
4. Dot liberally with margarine, place in moderate oven and cook until soft and golden

Serves 4

SWEET PASTRY

2 cups plain flour
½ teaspoon salt
2 tablespoons icing sugar
155 g (5 oz) polyunsaturated margarine
3 tablespoons iced water

METHOD

1. Sift flour, salt and icing sugar into a bowl and rub in the polyunsaturated margarine until mixture resembles fine breadcrumbs
2. Add small amounts of iced water and mix into pastry dough with a knife
3. Divide into half and roll out each piece on a lightly floured board

Sufficient pastry for two 20 cm (8 inch) pie shells or one double-crust pie

Sauces, spreads, dressings and mayonnaises, besides adding to the appearance and flavour of foods, are also an excellent method of including extra polyunsaturated fats.

Use white sauces for: basis for creamed soups; garnish for vegetables, fish, poultry and meat; basis for fish cakes, etc.

Use spreads for: making savoury breads; garnishes for cooked vegetables; spreading bread or toast used as bases for appetizers.

Use dressings for: raw salad greens, coleslaw, sliced tomato and cucumber; cooked string beans, asparagus, broccoli; marinading and basting meat, fish and poultry.

Use mayonnaises for: potato, rice or macaroni salads; on cooked vegetables such as broccoli, asparagus and cauliflower; on poached or fried fish; in salmon or tuna salads; salad of cooked chicken or veal with vegetables; on raw salad greens.

BARBECUE SAUCE

½ cup finely chopped onion
2 tablespoons brown sugar
1 teaspoon salt
1 teaspoon mustard
Pinch cayenne pepper
1 tablespoon Worcestershire sauce
3 tablespoons vinegar
½ cup tomato sauce
1 cup water
3 tablespoons mustard pickle

METHOD

1. Combine all ingredients in a saucepan and stir until well mixed
2. Simmer for 15 minutes
3. Serve hot with barbecue meats, sausages, meat loaves or fish

Makes 1¼ cups

BOILED SALAD DRESSING

2 tablespoons polyunsaturated margarine
60 g (2 oz) flour
2½ cups skim milk
½ cup polyunsaturated oil
1 teaspoon salt
Pepper
150 ml (5 fl oz) vinegar (tarragon preferably)
1½ tablespoons French mustard

METHOD

1. Melt margarine in saucepan, add half the flour and blend well
2. Blend remainder of flour with milk, removing lumps
3. Remove cooked margarine and flour from heat and add liquid all at once, stirring constantly
4. Return to heat and stir till mixture boils and thickens
5. Remove from heat and gradually beat in the oil, then fold in salt, pepper, vinegar and mustard
6. Bottle and keep in refrigerator

N.B. May need diluting with skim milk before use

Makes approximately 3¾ cups

Per 1¼ cups: 45 ml (1½ fl oz) oil

FRENCH DRESSING

3 tablespoons polyunsaturated oil
1 tablespoon vinegar
Salt, freshly ground pepper to taste
1 teaspoon sugar
½ teaspoon French mustard
1 small clove crushed garlic

METHOD

1. Place all ingredients in screwtop jar and shake thoroughly until blended
2. Store in refrigerator. Shake well before using

Per serve: 1 tablespoon oil   Serves 4

GARLIC SPREAD

125 g (4 oz) polyunsaturated margarine
2 cloves crushed garlic
Pepper and salt

METHOD

1. Cream margarine, garlic, seasoning until well blended
2. Store in refrigerator in airtight container

VARIATIONS

Parsley spread: Omit garlic. Add 1 tablespoon chopped parsley
Herb spread: Omit garlic. Add 1–2 teaspoons dried mixed herbs or 1 tablespoon finely chopped chives, tarragon, thyme, etc.

PIQUANT SAUCE

2 tablespoons tomato sauce
2 tablespoons Worcestershire sauce
1 tablespoon vinegar
2 tablespoons polyunsaturated oil
2 teaspoons sugar

METHOD

1. Place all ingredients in screwtop jar and shake thoroughly until blended
2. Store in refrigerator. Shake before using

Per tablespoon sauce: 2 teaspoons oil minimum

TARTARE SAUCE

1¼ cups polyunsaturated mayonnaise, or
boiled dressing (p. 80)
1 tablespoon chopped gherkin
Juice of ½ lemon
¼ teaspoon finely chopped herbs
1 teaspoon chopped capers
1 teaspoon white or tarragon vinegar
1 tablespoon chopped parsley

METHOD

1. Stir all ingredients into mayonnaise
2. Can be stored in refrigerator in screwtop jar

Per tablespoon sauce: 3 teaspoons oil

TARRAGON DRESSING

125 g (4 oz) polyunsaturated margarine
1 teaspoon tarragon vinegar
1 teaspoon lemon juice
¼ teaspoon Tabasco sauce
2 tablespoons polyunsaturated mayonnaise
Salt and freshly ground pepper to taste

METHOD

1. Blend all ingredients and season to taste
2. Spoon into serving bowl, cover and chill until needed

Per tablespoon dressing: 1 tablespoon oil equivalent

WHITE SAUCES

POURING SAUCE: Use as a foundation for soup

1 tablespoon polyunsaturated margarine
1 tablespoon plain flour
1¼ cups skim milk
3 tablespoons polyunsaturated oil
Salt and pepper to taste

METHOD

1. Melt margarine in saucepan but do not allow to boil
2. Remove from heat, add flour, salt and pepper and stir until smooth. Stir over heat for 1 minute but do not allow it to brown. Remove from heat
3. Add skim milk at once then return to hotplate and stir continually until sauce boils and thickens
4. Continue cooking with hotplate switched off for 2–3 minutes
5. Gradually add polyunsaturated oil, beating well after each addition. Season with salt and pepper

Per tablespoon sauce: 1 teaspoon oil

COATING SAUCE: Use with vegetables as sauce and in scalloped dishes

1 tablespoon polyunsaturated margarine
2 tablespoons plain flour
1¼ cups skim milk
3 tablespoons polyunsaturated oil
Salt and pepper to taste

METHOD

As for Pouring Sauce
Per tablespoon sauce: 1 teaspoon oil

VARIATIONS

Add to every 1¼ cups of sauce
Anchovy sauce: 1 tablespoon anchovy essence or ½ tin mashed anchovy fillets
Caper sauce: 1 tablespoon chopped capers and few drops vinegar
Parsley sauce: 1 tablespoon finely chopped parsley
Boiled onion sauce: ½ cup chopped boiled onion
Tomato cream sauce: 2 tablespoons tomato paste
Horseradish sauce: 1 tablespoon horseradish relish
Sweet white sauce: 1 tablespoon sugar, vanilla essence to flavour

THICK SAUCE: Use as foundation for savoury fillings

2 tablespoons polyunsaturated margarine
3 tablespoons plain flour
1¼ cups skim milk
3 tablespoons polyunsaturated oil
Salt and pepper to taste

METHOD

As for Pouring Sauce
Per tablespoon sauce: 1 teaspoon oil

PANADA SAUCE: Use as foundation for croquettes, fish cakes, etc.

4 tablespoons flour
1 cup skim milk
3 tablespoons polyunsaturated oil
Salt and pepper to taste

METHOD

1. Blend flour with skim milk
2. Bring slowly to boil, stirring constantly
3. Cook for few minutes
4. Season with salt and pepper

Per cup sauce: $\frac{1}{4}$ cup oil

BEVERAGES

Because saturated fats must be reduced, all forms of full cream milk must be avoided whether in the form of homogenized, pasteurized, evaporated, condensed or dried full cream milk.

Cream must not be used in coffee.

The use of skim milk (i.e. milk from which the cream has been removed) is unrestricted. Skim milk may be used as a drink, with cereals and in soups or white sauces. Buttermilk and low-fat yoghurt may be substituted for skim milk.

BUTTERMILK PUNCH

3 cups chilled buttermilk
$\frac{3}{4}$ cup orange juice
$1\frac{1}{2}$ tablespoons lemon juice
$1\frac{1}{2}$ tablespoons sugar
$\frac{1}{2}$ teaspoon cinnamon
$\frac{1}{2}$ teaspoon nutmeg

METHOD

1. Combine ingredients, beat until blended
2. Pour into chilled glasses
3. Garnish each with a thin orange slice and a sprig of fresh mint

Serves 4

CHOCOLATE MILK SHAKE

1¼ cups 'filled milk' (see below)
2 teaspoons chocolate flavour
Sugar – if desired
Polyunsaturated ice cream – if desired (p. 75)

METHOD

Mix all ingredients together in blender, milk shake attachment or with egg whisk

VARIATIONS

Banana: ½ banana + nutmeg to taste
Passionfruit: 1 passionfruit

'FILLED MILK'

2½ cups skim milk
3 tablespoons polyunsaturated oil

METHOD

1. Pour skim milk into screwtop bottle or covered jug
2. Add oil
3. Store in refrigerator
4. Shake well before using

May be used with cereals at breakfast or as plain milk drink. When used in tea or coffee the oil forms droplets on top of the beverage

Per cup milk: 6 teaspoons oil

ICE COFFEE

150 ml (5 fl oz) cold strong black coffee
150 ml (5 fl oz) cold skim milk
1–2 tablespoons polyunsaturated oil
4 tablespoons polyunsaturated ice cream (p. 75)
1 tablespoon sugar
¼ teaspoon vanilla essence
Cinnamon

METHOD

1. Mix all ingredients together in food blender or milk shake attachment until thick and foamy
2. Add extra ice cream, sprinkle with cinnamon and serve

MOCHA CREAM

2 teaspoons sugar
2 teaspoons cocoa
30 ml (1 fl oz) cold strong black coffee or
2 teaspoons instant coffee powder
280 ml (9 fl oz) cold skim milk
1–2 tablespoons polyunsaturated oil
4 tablespoons polyunsaturated ice cream
¼ teaspoon vanilla essence

METHOD

1. Blend cocoa and sugar with a little skim milk. Stir in remaining skim milk
2. Mix all ingredients in food blender, milk shake attachment, or with egg whisk until thick and foamy
3. Add extra ice cream and serve

MISCELLANEOUS
(APPETIZERS, FRITTERS, PASTRY, SANDWICH FILLINGS, ETC.)

Some foods commonly used as appetizers are very high in cholesterol and should not be eaten, e.g. egg yolks, oysters, lobster and fish roe. Other seafoods, e.g. crab and prawns are moderately high in cholesterol and may be eaten occasionally.

Cottage cheese, low fat yoghurt and buttermilk are made from skim milk and therefore have very little fat and consequently very little saturated fat and cholesterol. These foods may be eaten as frequently as desired. However, all other milk products, i.e. cheese, cream and butter are best avoided.

Avocado and olives contain more saturated than polyunsaturated fat and it is recommended that these foods only be eaten very occasionally. All nuts contain some polyunsaturated fat although the amount varies with the variety of nut. Walnuts, having the highest proportion of polyunsaturated fat are especially recommended for inclusion in the Modified Fat Diet.

Also recommended as appetizers because of their high content of polyunsaturated fats are eel, herrings, sardines, pilchards, sild, salmon and anchovies.

By the use of croutons, bread shapes and bread cases as bases for savouries, the amount of polyunsaturated fats eaten per day may be increased.

Safflower oil is the preferred base for all dressings because of its high polyunsaturated fat content. Olive oil and peanut oil are not recommended because of their low polyunsaturated fat content.

PARTY BREAD CASES

1 loaf fresh sliced bread
125 g (4 oz) melted polyunsaturated margarine

METHOD

1. Remove crusts from bread and brush both sides of bread lightly with melted margarine and press into deep patty tins
2. Bake in moderate oven for 15 minutes until golden brown
3. Some suggestions for filling:
   Devilled nuts (p. 89), sweet and sour tuna (p. 34), devilled chicken (p. 115)

CROUTONS

1 loaf sliced bread
polyunsaturated oil

METHOD

1. Cut bread slices into cubes, squares, triangles, circles or fancy shapes
2. Deep fry in oil until golden brown. Drain

May be used as garnish for soups, creamed dishes and as bases for savouries

COTTAGE CHEESE DIPS

125 g (4 oz) cottage cheese
45 g (1½ oz) polyunsaturated margarine
2 teaspoons skim milk

1. Beat cheese and margarine until light and very smooth, then beat in skim milk
2. Add selected flavouring. Chill 1 hour before use

FLAVOURINGS
Chives and cucumber: 1 tablespoon chopped and well-drained cucumber, 1 teaspoon salt, pinch cayenne pepper, chopped chives
Horseradish: ¼ teaspoon salt, 2 teaspoons bottled horseradish, pinch cayenne
French onion: 3 tablespoons French onion soup
Herb: 1 clove garlic crushed, 2 teaspoons grated onion, ¼ teaspoon salt, pinch mustard, ¼ cup polyunsaturated mayonnaise, ¼ teaspoon thyme, dash Tabasco sauce. Omit skim milk
Caraway and capers: 2 teaspoons capers, 1 tablespoon caraway seeds, 1 teaspoon finely grated onion
Celery: 2 teaspoons finely grated onion, 1 teaspoon Worcestershire sauce, 2 tablespoons chopped celery, salt and pepper
Gherkin: Dash paprika, 2 gherkins chopped, 1 tablespoon onion, salt and pepper
Pineapple savoury: 2 tablespoons crushed pineapple well drained, 2 tablespoons finely chopped walnuts
Curried salmon: 1 teaspoon curry powder, salt, pepper, 4 tablespoons salmon, 1 tablespoon finely chopped onions

COTTAGE CHEESE NUT BALLS

125 g (4 oz) cottage cheese
Cayenne pepper
1 tablespoon chopped gherkins
Chopped walnuts

METHOD
1. Combine cottage cheese and chopped gherkins and season with cayenne pepper
2. Roll into balls and toss in chopped nuts
3. Chill at least one hour before serving

DEVILLED WALNUTS

4 tablespoons chopped walnuts
45 g (1½ oz) polyunsaturated margarine
6 tablespoons cottage cheese
3 tablespoons chopped parsley
2 tablespoons chutney
Salt and cayenne pepper
Chilli strips
Party bread cases (p. 87)

METHOD
1. Sauté walnuts in margarine
2. Mix in cheese, parsley, chutney, salt and cayenne
3. Fill bread cases. Reheat before serving and garnish with chilli strips

FILLINGS FOR ROLLS AND SANDWICHES

Chicken and Celery: Equal parts of minced chicken and celery, seasoned with salt and moistened with a little polyunsaturated mayonnaise or boiled dressing (p. 80). Rabbit or fish may be substituted for the chicken

Peanut Butter and Onion: Beat together 1 cup peanut butter and 3 tablespoons polyunsaturated mayonnaise or boiled dressing (p. 80) and 1 tablespoon finely chopped onion

Salmon and Cucumber: Flake the salmon, blend with polyunsaturated mayonnaise or boiled dressing (p. 80). Add grated cucumber and mix. Season with a little salt and lemon juice. Tuna may replace the salmon

Cottage Cheese and Gherkins: Blend polyunsaturated margarine into cottage cheese until it is a 'creamy' consistency. Add chopped gherkins. Any combination of the following, may replace gherkins: chopped celery, walnuts, tomato, cucumber, onion, chicken, rabbit or fish

Walnuts, Raisins and Orange: Mix 2 tablespoons chopped raisins, 2 tablespoons chopped walnuts and grated rind of one orange. Moisten with polyunsaturated mayonnaise

FRITTER BATTER

1 cup flour
Pinch salt
1 tablespoon polyunsaturated oil
150 ml (5 fl oz) tepid water
(2 parts cold, 1 part boiling)
White of 1 egg

METHOD

1. Sift flour and salt into basin. Make a well in centre
2. Pour in oil. Stir flour in gradually with the back of a wooden spoon and add water, a little at a time, beating to a smooth batter
3. Beat egg white stiffly and fold it in very lightly just before using

This batter can be used to coat pineapple, fish pieces, banana, apple, corn, meat pieces, chicken pieces, etc.

GARLIC BREAD

Garlic spread (p. 81)
1 French loaf

METHOD

1. Cut diagonally through top to within 1 cm ($\frac{1}{2}$ inch) from base to give fingers of bread
2. Spread garlic spread thickly between fingers
3. Wrap loaf in foil and place in moderate oven for about 15–20 minutes

VARIATIONS

Herb bread: Use herb spread (p. 81)
Parsley bread: Use parsley spread (p. 81)

FRIED CRUMBS

2 cups soft white breadcrumbs
100 ml (3 fl oz) polyunsaturated oil

1. Heat oil, add breadcrumbs, tossing continually until golden brown
2. Drain on absorbent paper. Store in airtight container. Makes approximately 1½ cups

LENTEN VEGETABLE PIE

2 cups sliced tomatoes
1 cup onion rings
1½ cups cooked macaroni
1 cup cottage cheese
salt and pepper
1 teaspoon mixed dried herbs (optional)
2 teaspoons chopped parsley
75 g (2½ oz) polyunsaturated margarine
1 cup mashed pumpkin
1 cup S.R. flour
skim milk if required

METHOD

1. Place layers of tomato, onion, macaroni, cottage cheese, herbs and parsley into a 20 cm (8 inch) pie plate
2. Pour 60 g (2 oz) melted margarine over vegetables and season to taste
3. Place in a moderate oven and bake until vegetables are cooked
4. Mash pumpkin, add 15 g (½ oz) margarine and flour and mix to a stiff dough using skim milk if required
5. Roll out on a floured board to fit a 20 cm (8 inch) pie plate and place on filling
6. Brush with milk and bake in a hot oven for 15–20 minutes

Per serve: 2 teaspoons oil equivalent   Serves 4

PIZZA PIE

500 g (1 lb) fresh tomatoes
1 clove crushed garlic
½ cup polyunsaturated oil
Salt and pepper to taste
1 tin anchovy fillets

$\frac{1}{2}$ *cup cottage cheese*
6 sliced stuffed olives
2 cups S.R. flour
$\frac{1}{2}$ *teaspoon salt*
$\frac{2}{3}$ *cup skim milk*

METHOD

1. Peel and chop tomatoes. Place in pan with half the oil and garlic. Season with salt and pepper
2. Simmer gently for 30 minutes
3. Sift flour and salt into basin and add skim milk and remainder of oil
4. Stir with knife until it forms soft dough
5. Knead until dough is smooth and soft. Roll out and line a greased 23 cm (9 inch) tart plate
6. Fill with tomato mixture then top with anchovy fillets, sliced olives and cottage cheese
7. Bake in a moderate oven 40–45 minutes

Per serve: 30 ml (1 fl oz) oil   Serves 4

SAVOURY PASTRY

2 cups plain flour
1 teaspoon salt
$\frac{1}{2}$ *cup polyunsaturated oil*
$\frac{1}{2}$ *cup iced water*

METHOD

1. Sift flour and salt into basin
2. Beat together oil and water until thickened
3. Pour all at once into flour and mix with fork until flour is entirely moistened
4. Form pastry into a ball
5. Cut in half and roll out one piece at a time between two sheets of waxed paper, rolling out lightly from centre
6. Peel off top paper, lift paper and pastry by corners and place paper side up in a 20 cm (8 inch) pie plate
7. Remove remaining paper, ease pastry into pie plate
8. Fill with desired filling and repeat the above with second half of pastry. Seal the edges and flute; prick for steam to escape

9. Bake in hot oven for 15 minutes, reduce heat to moderate and continue baking a further 20 minutes (or according to time required for filling used)

N.B. Sufficient pastry for two 20 cm (8 inch) tart shells or one double crust pie

Suggested fillings: Savoury mince (p. 40); salmon wizz (p. 33)

SPANISH TART

$\frac{3}{4}$ *cup flour*
$\frac{3}{4}$ *cup S.R. flour*
$\frac{1}{4}$ *teaspoon salt*
125 g (4 oz) polyunsaturated margarine
cold water to mix

Filling:
Chopped parsley
2 tablespoons polyunsaturated oil
$\frac{3}{4}$ *cup sliced onions*
1 clove garlic crushed
3 small courgettes sliced
3 tomatoes peeled and sliced
salt and pepper

METHOD

1. Sift flours and salt into bowl, rub margarine in lightly with fingertips
2. Sprinkle enough water over to mix to a firm dough. Knead lightly
3. Chill 30 minutes then roll out thinly on floured board to fit a 20 cm (8 inch) greased flan ring
4. Bake in moderately hot oven for 12–15 minutes
5. Filling: Heat oil, add onions, garlic and courgettes. Fry lightly for 5 minutes (do not brown), add tomatoes and cook a further 3 minutes. Season to taste
6. Spoon hot filling into flan and serve sprinkled with parsley
7. Serve hot as a first course or for a light meal with a tossed salad

Per serve: 2 teaspoons oil   Serves 4

MENU FROM AUSTRALIA FOR MODIFIED FAT DIET

	BREAKFAST	LUNCH	DINNER
SUNDAY	Stewed peaches Porridge and 'filled milk' (85) Baked beans in tomato sauce on toast	French onion soup (28) Croutons (87) Roast seasoned leg lamb (40) Gravy Scalloped potato (55) Roast pumpkin Broccoli Apple strudel (68) and ice cream (75)	Pizza pie (91) Tossed salad Fresh fruit
MONDAY	Orange juice Porridge and 'filled milk' (85) Grilled fish, lemon wedges	Cold seasoned lamb slices Italian salad (59) lettuce Fresh fruit **or** Packed lunch (as above)	Rabbit casserole (51) Glazed potato (54) Minted peas Carrot straws Cinnamon crumble (73), custard (74)
TUESDAY	Grapefruit Cereal and 'filled milk' (85) Asparagus with parsley spread (81) on toast	Salmon wizz (33) Tomato slices Fresh fruit **or** Packed lunch Tomato salmon and onion sandwiches Cottage cheese and cucumber sandwiches Fresh fruit	Corned silverside, onion sauce (83) Boiled potatoes Cabbage Tomato scallop (56) Chocolate sauce pudding (72)

Day	Breakfast	Lunch	Dinner
WEDNESDAY	Pineapple juice Porridge and 'filled milk' (85) Spaghetti in tomato sauce on toast	Cold silverside Tomato, marinaded cucumber (59) Cottage cheese potato salad (58) Fresh fruit **or** Packed lunch (as above)	Fried chicken pieces (90) Mashed potato Corn, beans Creamed rice (74) + canned cherries
THURSDAY	Stewed prunes Cereal and 'filled milk' (85) Grilled kippers and lemon juice, parsley spread (81)	Chilled tomato soup (26) Peanut butter and celery sandwiches Raisin and walnut (89) sandwiches Fresh fruit **or** Packed lunch (as above)	Malaysian lamb curry (39) Saffron rice (54) Quick banana dessert (78)
FRIDAY	Fruit compote Cereal and 'filled milk' (85) Sweet corn niblets on toast	Spanish tart (93) Tossed salad + piquant sauce (81) Fresh fruit **or** Packed lunch Tuna and gherkin sandwich (89) Yoghurt Fresh fruit	Seasoned fillet of fish (34) Baked jacket potatoes Beans Ice cream (75) and fresh fruit salad
SATURDAY	Tomato juice Cereal and 'filled milk' (85) Grilled tomato on toast	Spaghetti + meat sauce (112) Cabbage salad (58) Fresh fruit	Veal and potato casserole (44) Corn, brussels sprouts Lemon meringue pie (76)

6
IF YOU HAVE A
WEIGHT PROBLEM

Weight reduction primarily aims to bring about a reduction in body fatness. At the same time it should aim to correct faulty eating habits and to establish new eating patterns which can be maintained after an ideal body weight is attained.

Although reduction in fatness invariably results in a decrease in body weight, it should be remembered that water, bone and all the other tissues of the body, including muscle, make their contribution to the total weight of the body. In general, however, any 'excess' body weight, that is, weight over and above what is regarded as 'ideal' or desirable for a person's height and sex (Table, page 97) is a measure of the amount of excess fat carried in the body. It is usual for weight to fluctuate continuously due mainly to variations in the water content of the body. Even when body fat is being lost successfully, the body weight may remain stationary or even rise over a short period; in the long term, however, the trend will be downwards. Unless you are aware of this, you may be unnecessarily disheartened.

To lose fat is a slow process. You cannot hope to lose more than one kilogram (two pounds) of body fat per week, even though the initial loss of body weight is sometimes more impressive. A steady loss of three kilograms (half a stone) per month would be a highly successful result.

The essential feature of any weight reducing programme is to eat less or exercise more or to do both.

Two dietary programmes are described on pages 98–99 for weight reduction. One is a simple, rough-and-ready scheme. The other is more rigid and detailed and is set out in two parts, depending on whether or not weight reduction is to be combined with reduction of the blood cholesterol level by modifying the fats in the diet. The programme should be used only when there are no complicating conditions. Diabetics, pregnant women, parents of obese children, people who are grossly overweight and those who have any sort of medical complaint, should consult their doctor before commencing any weight reducing programme. A doctor should also be consulted if the intention is to reduce weight drastically or to continue weight reduction over a long period of time.

Finally, a selection of recipes and a week's menus for the weight reducing and weight-plus-cholesterol reducing programmes are included to show that meals need not be uninteresting.

DESIRABLE WEIGHT
ACCORDING TO HEIGHT AND SEX
(without shoes and wearing ordinary clothing)

HEIGHT			WEIGHT			
			MEN		WOMEN	
cm	ft in		kg	st lbs	kg	st lbs
147.4	4	10			47.6	7 7
149.9	4	11	55.3	8 10	49.0	7 10
152.4	5	0	56.7	8 13	50.8	8 0
155.0	5	1	58.1	9 2	52.2	8 3
157.5	5	2	59.9	9 6	53.5	8 6
160.1	5	3	61.7	9 10	54.9	8 9
162.6	5	4	63.0	9 13	56.7	8 13
165.1	5	5	64.4	10 2	58.5	9 3
167.7	5	6	65.8	10 5	59.9	9 6
170.2	5	7	67.6	10 9	61.7	9 10
172.8	5	8	69.4	10 13	63.5	10 0
175.3	5	9	71.2	11 3	65.3	10 4
177.8	5	10	73.0	11 7	67.6	10 9
180.4	5	11	75.3	11 12	69.9	11 0
182.9	6	0	77.1	12 2		
185.5	6	1	78.9	12 6		
188.0	6	2	80.8	12 10		
190.5	6	3	82.1	12 13		

10% under or over the desirable weight can be considered a reasonable margin.

DIETS FOR WEIGHT REDUCTION: A SIMPLE SCHEME

(i) Eat less by consciously taking smaller helpings and cutting away the fat.

(ii) Choose foods which supply fewer calories per serving.

(iii) Increase physical activity – walk to the next bus stop, walk upstairs, stand rather than sit, do exercises, take up sport. Patients with medical complications should check with their doctor.

(iv) Check progress by weighing weekly.

Protein, fat, carbohydrates and alcohol all supply calories or fuel for energy expenditure but fats are the richest source of calories. Fats include butter, cream, margarines, oils, lard, dripping and similar frying mediums. Food items which use both fat and carbohydrates in their preparation are rich in calories, e.g. fried foods, cakes, pastries, biscuits. Beer, wines, sugar, sweetened cordials and soft drinks are not essential foods and they are often to blame for excess calories. Essential foods mean those foods which are regarded as rich sources of proteins, vitamins and minerals, i.e. meat, milk, fruit and cereals.

No foods are forbidden to you in this programme, but there should be a reduction in the number of times calorie rich foods are eaten each week. If you elect to follow this type of diet programme then on most occasions you should substitute a lower calorie food item for the higher calorie food, i.e. grilled for fried meats; fruit for biscuits, cakes and puddings; and spirits plus water or soda for beer.

ENERGY RESTRICTED DIETS

This diet programme is designed to provide fewer calories than are used in normal daily activities; strict adherence to it will certainly result in weight reduction. Some foods are prohibited (calorie rich foods), some are limited (foods required to ensure an adequate intake of essential nutrients, i.e. protein, vitamins and minerals) and others are unrestricted (low calorie foods).

Details of two diets, each of which provide 1200 kcal. per day, are given below. If you are concerned only with reducing weight then follow the dietary programme outlined in Diet No. 1. (See also menu on page 134.)

Diet No. 2 is to be followed if blood cholesterol is to be reduced at the same time. (See also menu on page 136.) The principles to be followed in this latter diet programme are the same as those outlined in the Modified Fat Diet with the additional requirement of restricting your calorie intake. For further details of these principles read the section on the Modified Fat Diet (p. 18).

FOODS ALLOWED EACH DAY	DIET NO. 1	DIET NO. 2
MILK	300 ml (10 fl oz) full cream milk	300 ml (10 fl oz) skim milk
EGG	One	None
BEEF, LAMB, PORK	150 g (5 oz) cooked weight (i.e. 2 portions)	60 g (2 oz) cooked weight lamb, beef, no pork
POULTRY, RABBIT	As a meat substitute	125 g (4 oz) cooked weight
FISH	As a meat substitute	As a meat substitute
CHEESE	As a meat or milk substitute	Only cottage cheese allowed as a meat or milk substitute
FRUIT	2 portions	Same
'STARCHY' VEGETABLES	3 portions	Same
'NON-STARCHY' VEGETABLES	As desired	Same
BREAD	90 g (3 oz)	Same
BUTTER	15 g (½ oz)	None
POLYUNSATURATED MARGARINE	As a butter substitute	15 g (½ oz)
POLYUNSATURATED OIL	—	15 ml (½ fl oz)

FRUIT

Fruit and fruit juices contain carbohydrate in the form of sugars and if eaten in excess will supply extra calories. Use either fresh, stewed or canned fruit *without* sugar. Artificial sweeteners may be used if desired. Do not boil saccharine.

1 portion = 1 medium sized apple, pear, orange, peach
2 medium sized apricots, plums, nectarines
1 small banana or mango
12–14 cherries or grapes
100 ml (3 fl oz) fruit juice
½ cup blackberries, fresh fruit salad, paw-paw or pineapple
(1 cup = 250 ml [8 fl oz] standard measure cup)

The amount of sugar per portion in the following fruits is very low and so you may have one of them as an extra each day.

1 portion = ½ small grapefruit – no added sugar
1 average slice honeydew
1 large slice watermelon
1 glass tomato juice, 180 ml (6 fl oz)
1 passionfruit
Average quantity stewed rhubarb – no added sugar
Average quantity stewed gooseberries – no added sugar

'STARCHY' VEGETABLES

Vegetables which contain a larger proportion of carbohydrates, in the form of starch and sugar, and consequently supply more calories are referred to as the 'starchy' vegetables.

1 portion = ½ cup, 90 g (3 oz) by weight, beetroot, carrots, pumpkin
= ⅓ cup, 60 g (2 oz) by weight, broad beans, corn, parsnip, peas, potatoes

1 portion of fruit may be substituted for 1 portion of 'starchy' vegetables.

NON-STARCHY VEGETABLES

These vegetables contain a low proportion of carbohydrate and therefore supply few calories per serve. They may be used several times each day to add variety and to

satisfy hunger. They may also be used for 'nibbles' between meals:

Asparagus, french beans, broccoli, brussels sprouts, cabbage, cauliflower, celery, courgette, cucumber, egg
plant, kale, lettuce, marrow, mushrooms, onions, peppers (red or green capsicum), radishes, spinach, tomato,
tomato purée, turnips, watercress.

SUBSTITUTIONS

Weight reduction takes time and a monotonous diet is
both uninteresting and difficult to follow. There is no
reason why you should not have a varied menu and at the
same time lose weight. Study the *substitutions* below and
on most occasions a few adjustments should enable you to
have the same food as the rest of your family.

Foods within the following groups may be substituted or
exchanged for one another. Foods from *different* groups
cannot be substituted because they differ in their content
of protein, fat, carbohydrate and calories.

Milk substitutions:
150 ml (5 fl oz)
whole milk = 300 ml (10 fl oz) skim milk
300 ml (10 fl oz) buttermilk
150 g (5 oz) unflavoured yoghurt
150 g (5 oz) unflavoured non-fat
yoghurt
30 g (1 oz) cheese
90 g (3 oz) cottage cheese
60 g (2 oz) vanilla ice cream
150 ml (5 fl oz)
skim milk = 150 ml (5 fl oz) buttermilk
125 g (4 oz) unflavoured non-fat
yoghurt
60 g (2 oz) cottage cheese

Meat substitutions: All visible fat is to be removed *before
cooking*. Prepare meats without *flour*. Use butter, polyunsaturated margarine or oil from *daily allowance* for
cooking. No *extra* fats to be used.

30 g (1 oz)
cooked meat = 90 g (3 oz) steamed fish, water-pack
tuna or salmon
60 g (2 oz) fish + 1 teaspoon butter,
polyunsaturated margarine or polyunsaturated oil
30 g (1 oz) oil-pack fish, such as sardine
or tuna
30 g (1 oz) cheese (for use in Diet No. 1
only)
90 g (3 oz) cottage cheese
1 egg (for use in Diet No. 1 only)

Bread substitutions: Bread, plain white, brown, rye or
wholemeal. No fancy types.
30 g (1 oz) bread = 1 slice of 680 g (22 oz) sandwich cut
loaf

15 g ($\frac{1}{2}$ oz)
bread ($\frac{1}{2}$ slice) = 1 portion fruit
1 portion starchy vegetable
2 Vitaweat
1 rye crispbread
1 wheatmeal biscuit

30 g (1 oz)
bread (1 slice) = $\frac{1}{2}$ cup cooked cereal, i.e. rice, spaghetti,
macaroni, rolled oats
$\frac{3}{4}$ cup prepared cereal, i.e. rice krispies,
cornflakes

FOODS NOT ALLOWED

Sugar, honey, jam, marmalade; dried fruit; lollies, chocolates, cordials, syrups; nuts; cakes, pastries, biscuits, puddings, ice cream; flours, cornflour, arrowroot, thickened
soups, gravies and stews; salad dressings, mayonnaise, oil,
cream; fried foods; peanut butter; alcoholic drinks.

FOODS ALLOWED
IN UNLIMITED AMOUNTS

Barmene, bovril, clear broth (all fat removed), black tea
or coffee, condiments, curry powder, essences, herbs,
junket tablets, unsweetened lemon juice, low calorie

soft drinks, Marmite, mustard powder, spices, saccharine, sugarless cordials, sugarless (diabetic) jelly, soda water, vinegar, Worcestershire sauce, 'non-starchy' vegetables.

WHEN DINING OUT

Select menu from fruit juice or fruit cocktails, clear soup, grills, salads (no dressing); fruit or cheese as dessert.

SPECIAL DIET FOODS

These are mostly products in which sugar has been replaced by other sweetening agents such as glycerine, sorbitol or saccharine. Before buying any of these products check on the label to see which sweetening agent has been used. Products sweetened with glycerine and sorbitol, e.g. 'diabetic' chocolates and 'diabetic' jams are not recommended because both these sweetening agents are slowly absorbed and in being used by the body they produce as many calories per gram as ordinary sugar. Saccharine is not metabolized in the body and hence does not supply any calories. Examples of products using saccharine are soft drinks, cordials, and 'diabetic' jelly. 'Diabetic' canned fruits are allowed provided they are substituted for a portion of fresh fruit.

OTHER WEIGHT REDUCING PROGRAMMES

Other programmes which have been suggested at various times include 'gimmick' diets, fluid diets, and even complete starvation in which only vitamins and calorie-free fluids are taken.

When and if complete starvation is undertaken it should only be under strict medical supervision. Complete starvation may cause a large loss of muscle and other protein-containing tissues and may also precipitate gout, peptic ulceration and other complications.

'Gimmick' diets include those diets based on a particular food such as eggs, bananas, etc. Fluid diets, whether based on fruit juices or commercially prepared mixtures, are similar to the 'gimmick' diets in that they appeal to those people who like to try something different. These types of reducing diets are not recommended because usually they do not supply adequate amounts of all the essential nutrients which are required each day, they can only be tolerated for short periods and they do not train you in new food habits which you can continue after you attain your ideal body weight.

PROGRESS DURING WEIGHT REDUCTION

It is advisable not to weigh yourself more than once each week. Remember, as discussed earlier, that body weight can vary by as much as two kilograms (several pounds) from one day to the next or even within the one day due to changes in the amount of water in the body. Therefore do not become depressed if your weight remains stationary or increases over short periods even though you have adhered strictly to your diet. The amount of fat in the body will have decreased – and this is the main objective of the programme – and the general trend in body weight will be a reduction over the weeks and months. An average weekly loss of a half to one kilogram (one or two pounds) is as good as can be expected.

There is no advantage in restricting salt or water (or non-calorie drinks) unless the doctor has ordered this for other reasons.

WHEN WEIGHT REDUCTION IS STOPPED

Once you reach your goal you can relax your diet but it is still advisable to keep weekly checks on your weight. Your aim now is to maintain this new weight. This means that you will be able to relax your diet and eat more. Introduce extra foods gradually, watching your weight, but preserve the general features of the new food habits which you have acquired. Cautiously add small amounts of items which you have particularly missed, e.g. a little more lean meat, maybe thickened gravy, extra fruit or vegetable, or a dessert or piece of cake. Sugar is not recommended for reintroduction because it supplies only calories. During the first six months or so in particular, you must be very careful that you do not revert to your former eating habits because if you do you will start regaining all the weight you have lost.

7
INTRODUCTION TO RECIPES FOR CALORIE RESTRICTED DIETS

These recipes are included to show that meals on a Restricted Calorie Diet need not be uninteresting. By a few adaptations such as omitting fats and thickening agents and reducing the amount of stock normally used most of your favourite meat recipes become suitable for use while on this diet. Alcohol may be used in cooking. No recipes have been included for cakes, biscuits or fancy desserts because these are calorie-rich foods.

Information at the end of each recipe indicates if a substitution of one portion of fruit, 'starchy' vegetable or meat, etc. is required per serve. For example 'Substitution: I portion meat' means that each serve of that particular dish is equivalent to one of the two portions of meat allowed per day in the Restricted Calorie Diet. 'Substitution: Free' means there is no restriction on the number of serves eaten each day.

8
RECIPES FOR CALORIE RESTRICTED DIETS

SOUPS

ASPARAGUS SOUP

1 tin asparagus cuts, 250 g (8 oz)
60 g (2 oz) cold cooked chicken
2½ cups water
150 ml (5 fl oz) asparagus liquid
3 chicken cubes
1 teaspoon brandy or dry sherry (optional)
Salt and pepper

METHOD

Combine all ingredients, bring to boil

Substitution: Free   Serves 4

CELERY SOUP

4 cups beef stock
2 cups finely chopped celery
2 teaspoons Marmite or Barmene
Salt and pepper

METHOD

Add chopped celery, Marmite or Barmene, salt and pepper to stock and heat gently for 10 minutes

Substitution: Free   Serves 4

CHILLED BUTTERMILK SOUP

425 ml (15 fl oz) canned tomato juice
2 cups chilled buttermilk
Chopped chives or shallots
Salt and pepper

METHOD

1. Blend juice and buttermilk, add chives or shallots
2. Season to taste. Chill

Substitution: 120 ml (4 fl oz) skim milk   Serves 4

CHINESE CHICKEN SOUP

60 g (2 oz) raw chicken cut into strips
2 teaspoons salt
4–6 dried Chinese mushrooms
4 cups chicken stock
2 teaspoons soy sauce
1 tablespoon lemon juice
Chopped chives

METHOD

1. Sprinkle chicken strips with salt and set aside
2. Add dried mushrooms to 1 cup hot chicken stock and allow to stand
3. Add remainder of stock to saucepan plus soy sauce and bring to the boil
4. Remove mushrooms from stock and cut into thin strips
5. Add mushrooms, chicken strips and stock to remainder of stock and simmer for 5–10 minutes
6. Add lemon juice and chives and simmer further 5 minutes

Substitution: Free   Serves 4

JULIENNE SOUP

½ cup onions
¼ cup carrots
¼ cup turnips
4 cups beef stock
½ cup green beans (fresh or tinned)
Salt and pepper to taste

METHOD

1. Slice the onions finely, cut carrots and turnips into matchsticks and simmer in the stock until tender
2. Add beans and salt and pepper to taste

Substitution: Free   Serves 4

TOMATO CONSOMMÉ

425 ml (15 fl oz) canned tomato juice
1 beef cube
1¼ cups water
Squeeze lemon juice
Salt and pepper to taste

METHOD

1. Combine all ingredients and serve piping hot

Substitution: Free   Serves 4

FISH

BAKED FISH

750 g (1½ lb) fish fillets
1 tablespoon lemon juice
1½ cups sliced tomatoes
¾ cup onion rings
Salt and pepper
Pinch mixed herbs (optional)

METHOD

1. Place fish on large piece of foil and sprinkle with lemon juice
2. Top with tomato slices, onion rings, salt, pepper and herbs
3. Tightly fold edges of foil, place on tray in moderate oven for 15–20 minutes or until cooked

Substitution: 1 portion meat   Serves 4

750 g (1½ lb) fish fillets
2 small cloves garlic thinly sliced
2 tablespoons chopped parsley
¼ teaspoon pepper
1 teaspoon salt
150 ml (5 fl oz) white vinegar

METHOD

1. Arrange fillets in baking dish
2. Combine garlic with pepper, salt and parsley, mix gradually with vinegar and pour over fish. Let stand 1 hour
3. Bake in moderate oven 15–20 minutes

Substitution: 1 portion meat   Serves 4

QUICK SALMON SNACK

2 tablespoons Worcestershire sauce
4 tablespoons tomato sauce (p. 131) or
tomato purée
2 teaspoons chilli sauce
1 teaspoon cayenne pepper
Salt
425 g (15 oz) tin salmon

METHOD

1. Combine all sauce ingredients together, stir well
2. Drain and flake salmon and fold through sauce
3. Place in fancy mould or basin and chill. May also be served hot

Substitution: 1 portion meat   Serves 4

SALMON AND TOMATO SAVOURY

2 cups chopped tomato
½ cup onion rings
1 tablespoon lemon juice
½ cup green pepper rings
½ teaspoon mustard

$\frac{1}{4}$ *teaspoon pepper*
$\frac{1}{2}$ *teaspoon salt*
1 dessertspoon chopped parsley
425 g (15 oz) tin salmon

METHOD

1. Mix together tomatoes, onions, lemon juice, capsicum, mustard, pepper, salt and parsley. Cook until tender
2. Add flaked salmon
3. Simmer until salmon is heated, about 5–10 minutes

Substitution: 1 portion meat   Serves 4

VARIATION

Tuna and tomato savoury: Substitute tuna for salmon

SOUSED FISH

750 g (1$\frac{1}{2}$ lb) fish fillets
1 cup sliced onion
6 peppercorns
6 cloves
2 bay leaves
1 teaspoon salt
2 cups vinegar
1 lettuce

METHOD

1. Prepare fish and cut in slices
2. Place fish slices in a baking dish and cover with sliced onion
3. Add dry ingredients, then the vinegar and cover with greased paper
4. Bake in a moderately hot oven for 30 minutes
5. Let fish stand in liquor till set then lift out fish carefully and place in centre of serving dish
6. Strain liquor over fish and garnish with lettuce leaves

Substitution: 1 portion meat   Serves 4

BRAISED CHOPS

500 g (1 lb) lean chump chops
½ cup chopped celery
1 cup chopped onion
½ cup chopped green pepper
1 bay leaf
2 teaspoons vinegar
2 teaspoons soy sauce
½ cup beef stock
Salt and pepper to taste
1 tablespoon chopped parsley

METHOD

1. Trim chops of fat. Arrange in baking dish
2. Add celery, onion, peppers, bay leaf, vinegar, soy sauce, stock, salt and pepper
3. Bake in moderate oven for approximately 2 hours or until the chops are tender
4. Serve sprinkled with parsley

Substitution: 1 portion meat   Serves 4

BRAISED STEAK

500 g (1 lb) braising steak
1 cup chopped onions
1 cup chopped celery
½ cup chopped green pepper
1 cup chopped tomatoes
¾ cup stock
½ teaspoon salt

METHOD

1. Trim meat of fat, cut into serving pieces and place in casserole dish
2. Add vegetables and pour stock over meat
3. Cook in a moderate oven until meat is tender; add more stock if required

Substitution: 1 portion meat   Serves 4

INDIAN BEEF MARINADE

500 g (1 lb) lean topside cut into thin strips
2 teaspoons powdered coriander
1 teaspoon cumin
2 teaspoons turmeric
1½ tablespoons green ginger cut as match sticks
2 cloves crushed garlic
2 cups chopped onions
¾ cup vinegar
1 bay leaf
Salt

METHOD

1. Mix together spices, crushed garlic and onions and blend into vinegar
2. Pour over beef slices and allow to marinade for 24 hours, turning often
3. Simmer meat in marinade until meat is tender

Substitution: 1 portion meat   Serves 4

MEAT SAUCE

500 g (1 lb) minced meat
½ cup chopped onion
1 clove garlic
½ cup chopped green pepper
1 bay leaf
1 cup tomato juice or 1 cup chopped tomatoes
¼ teaspoon pepper
½ teaspoon salt

METHOD

1. Heat frypan or saucepan. Add meat, stirring constantly until it changes colour
2. Add onion, garlic and peppers and cook a further 5 minutes
3. Add bay leaf, tomato juice (or tomatoes), pepper and salt and cook gently for 20–30 minutes. Set aside to cool
4. Skim fat off. Reheat to serve

Substitution: 1 portion meat   Serves 4

MEXICAN RICE

500 g (1 lb) lean minced chuck steak
½ cup uncooked rice
¾ cup thinly sliced onion
1 small clove finely crushed garlic
2 teaspoons salt
1 tablespoon chilli powder or tomato chutney (p. 130)
⅓ cup tomato sauce (p. 131)
250 g (½ lb) skinned roughly chopped tomatoes
1 cup water or stock

METHOD

1. Place meat, rice, onion and garlic in saucepan and stir continuously until meat is brown
2. Add salt, chilli powder, tomato sauce, tomatoes and water; stir well
3. Cover, simmer 25 minutes, stirring occasionally or until rice is tender   Serves 4

Substitution: 1 portion meat + 30 g (1 oz) bread

N.B. When using recipe for *Restricted Calorie Diet* No. 2, fry rice in 60 ml (2 fl oz) polyunsaturated oil then continue as above.

Substitution: 1 portion meat + 30 g (1 oz) bread + 15 ml (½ fl oz) oil

STEAK DIANE

500 g (1 lb) rump steak cut thinly
3 tablespoons Worcestershire sauce
100 ml (3 fl oz) tomato juice
1½ tablespoons vinegar
1 tablespoon chopped parsley

METHOD

1. Sear steak quickly on both sides in large frying pan
2. Mix Worcestershire sauce, tomato juice and vinegar. Add to pan and bring to boil
3. Simmer with lid off until meat is tender and liquid has reduced
4. Sprinkle with chopped parsley before serving

Substitution: 1 portion meat   Serves 4

VEAL MARENGO

750 g (1½ lb) veal
1 clove crushed garlic
1 cup small tomato wedges
1 cup fine onion wedges
1 small tin button mushrooms
2 teaspoons tomato paste
150 ml (5 fl oz) dry white wine and
150 ml (5 fl oz) chicken stock, or
300 ml (10 fl oz) chicken stock
1 tablespoon chopped parsley

METHOD

1. Cut veal into serving pieces. Place in casserole dish
2. Add garlic, tomato, onion, mushrooms, tomato paste, wine and chicken stock
3. Cover and cook in moderate oven until tender – approximately 1½ hours; garnish with parsley

Substitution: 1 portion meat   Serves 4

POULTRY AND GAME

BRAISED RABBIT

750 g (1½ lb) rabbit pieces
¼ teaspoon pepper
½ teaspoon salt
Grated rind of 1 lemon
2 bay leaves
1 cup sliced tomatoes
1 cup sliced onions
1 cup chicken stock

METHOD

1. Arrange rabbit in baking dish and sprinkle with pepper, salt, lemon rind and bay leaves
2. Cover with tomato, onions and stock
3. Cover dish and bake in moderate oven for 1–1½ hours

Substitution: 1 portion meat   Serves 4

CHICKEN IN WINE

1 jointed 1.1 kg (2½ lb) chicken
1 tablespoon lemon juice
1 teaspoon salt
¼ teaspoon freshly ground black pepper
1 cup dry white wine
1 tablespoon chopped chives or onions
1 tablespoon parsley
Pinch dried thyme
Pinch dried tarragon

METHOD

1. Wash the chicken, dry thoroughly and rub all over with the lemon juice
2. Season with salt and pepper
3. Place chicken pieces, wine, chopped chives, parsley, thyme and tarragon in casserole dish
4. Cover and cook in moderate oven until chicken is tender

Substitution: 1 portion meat   Serves 4

DEVILLED CHICKEN

1.1 kg (2½ lb) chicken
½ cup chopped onion
½ cup chopped carrot
½ cup chopped turnip
Bouquet garni (parsley, thyme, marjoram and
bay leaf tied together with cotton)

METHOD

1. Simmer chicken with vegetables barely covered with chicken stock and bouquet garni until tender
2. Leave in the cooking liquor until cold, then skin, joint and remove leg bones, slice into convenient pieces
3. Lay pieces in a casserole, pour over Devil Sauce to moisten and place in a moderate oven. Heat for 15 minutes

Substitution: 1 portion meat   Serves 4

Devil Sauce

3 tablespoons Worcestershire sauce
2 tablespoons button mushrooms, sliced
1 tablespoon tarragon vinegar
1 tablespoon finely chopped onions
2 or 3 slices lemon cut in half
1 clove crushed garlic
1 teaspoon salt
1 cup strong chicken stock
1 cup tinned or fresh skinned chopped tomatoes
Freshly ground black pepper
1 bay leaf

METHOD

Simmer these ingredients 10 minutes, pour over chicken while hot

HAWAIIAN CHICKEN

1 chicken 1.0–1.1 kg (2–2½ lb) cut into pieces
¼ teaspoon salt
¼ teaspoon pepper
2 teaspoons dry mustard
¼ teaspoon grated nutmeg
1 cup chopped onions
2 tablespoons vinegar
425 g (15 oz) can unsweetened pineapple pieces
or 2 cups fresh pineapple pieces
1 cup chicken stock
1 tablespoon parsley

METHOD

1. Mix salt, pepper, mustard, nutmeg and rub over chicken pieces
2. Place in casserole dish, add onion, vinegar, pineapple pieces and stock
3. Cook in moderate oven till meat is tender, about 1½–2 hours
4. Garnish with parsley   Serves 4

Substitution: 1 portion meat + 1 portion fruit

RABBIT IN BARBECUE SAUCE

750 g (1½ lb) rabbit pieces
½ cup finely chopped onion
1 teaspoon salt
1 teaspoon mustard
Pinch cayenne pepper
1 tablespoon Worcestershire sauce
¼ cup vinegar
½ cup tomato sauce (p. 131)
1 cup water
Liquid sweetener to taste

METHOD

1. Place rabbit pieces in casserole dish
2. Combine all other ingredients and pour over rabbit pieces
3. Cook in moderate oven until rabbit is cooked, about 1½ hours

Substitution: 1 portion meat   Serves 4

VARIATIONS

Chicken, lean beef or fish fillets may replace the rabbit

VEGETABLES

BAKED ONIONS

4 medium sized onions
½ cup chicken stock
Salt and pepper

METHOD

1. Arrange prepared onions in baking dish and pour chicken stock over. Sprinkle with salt and pepper
2. Bake in moderate oven till tender   Serves 4

Substitution: Free

VARIATION

Potato or pumpkin may be cooked by this method
Substitution: 1 portion vegetable

SAVOURY MACARONI

75 g (2½ oz) macaroni
2 cups chopped tomato
¼ cup chopped green peppers
¼ cup chopped onion
1 clove garlic
1 tablespoon chopped parsley
Salt and pepper

METHOD

1. Cook macaroni in salted water. Drain
2. Cook tomatoes, pepper, onions and garlic together until soft
3. Season with salt and pepper
4. Mix sauce through macaroni and garnish with parsley

Substitution: 30 g (1 oz) bread   Serves 4

VARIATION

Rice or spaghetti may be substituted for macaroni

STUFFED TOMATOES

4 large tomatoes
125 g (4 oz) cooked fish, salmon or tuna
½ cup chopped onion
¼ cup chopped celery
Pinch tarragon
Salt and pepper

METHOD

1. Cut tops off tomatoes and scoop out centres
2. Add cooked fish, onion, celery, tarragon, salt and pepper to tomato pulp
3. Fill tomatoes with required amount of mixture and bake in moderate oven for 10–15 minutes

Substitution: Free

VARIATIONS

The flaked fish may be replaced by the following:

1. Savoury stuffed tomato: 2 tablespoons chopped green pepper
Substitution: Free
2. Minced stuffed tomato: 125 g (4 oz) chopped cold meat or 125 g (4 oz) lean mince
Substitution: 30 g (1 oz) meat
3. Anchovy stuffed tomato: 4 anchovy fillets chopped + 1 tablespoon parsley
Substitution: Free
4. Mushroom stuffed tomato: 1 cup chopped mushrooms
Substitution: Free

TOMATO AND ONION CASSEROLE

3 large or 6 small tomatoes
1 cup thin onion rings
1 teaspoon dried herbs
Salt and pepper

METHOD

1. Wash and slice tomatoes
2. Place layer of tomatoes in ovenproof dish, cover with onions, sprinkle with herbs, salt and pepper and repeat layers till dish is filled
3. Bake in moderate oven till vegetables are soft

Substitution: Free   Serves 4

SALADS

BEAN SALAD

2 cups sliced french beans
1 teaspoon mustard seeds
3 tablespoons malt vinegar
3 tablespoons water

METHOD

1. Cook beans and mustard seeds in boiling salted water. Drain
2. Combine vinegar and water, pour over beans, chill

Substitution: Free   Serves 4

COLESLAW

3 cups finely shredded cabbage
¼ cup finely shredded green pepper
¼ cup grated onion
¼ cup grated radish
1 teaspoon salt
¼ teaspoon pepper
Spiced dressing (p. 129)

METHOD

Toss cabbage lightly with green pepper, onion, radish, salt, pepper and dressing

Substitution: Free   Serves 4

GREEN BEAN RING

1 tablespoon gelatine
¼ cup cold water·
2 cups stock or water
2 teaspoons white vinegar
2 teaspoons lemon juice
¼ teaspoon pepper
½ teaspoon salt
½ teaspoon garlic salt
¼ cup chopped celery
1¾ cups cooked cut green beans

METHOD

1. Soften gelatine in water
2. Place stock in saucepan with vinegar, lemon juice, garlic salt, pepper, salt and celery
3. Heat gently till boiling then remove from heat and add softened gelatine, stir until dissolved
4. Add cooked beans, pour into 18 cm (7 inch) ring tin, 4 small ring moulds or recess tin
5. Chill 1 hour or till set. Run knife around edges to loosen

Substitution: Free   Serves 4

GREEN CABBAGE RELISH

½ large green cabbage
2 large onions
Salt
2½ cups vinegar
Liquid sweetener to taste
2 teaspoons curry powder
1 teaspoon mustard

METHOD

1. Clean cabbage and cut up very finely
2. Peel and cut onions finely
3. Fold through cabbage and sprinkle with enough salt to coat well and leave for 24 hours
4. Drain and rinse thoroughly and then put in the vinegar to which sweetener, mustard and curry powder have been added
5. Bring to boil and allow to simmer for 20 minutes
6. Bottle and seal. Serve with grilled meat and salads

Substitution: Free   Makes 2½–3¾ cups

PICKLED CUCUMBERS

4 large cucumbers
Brine, 750 g (1½ lb) salt to 5 cups water
Spiced vinegar (p. 129)

METHOD

1. Slice cucumbers, with skin on, very thinly
2. Quarter each slice or, if cucumber is small, leave in rings
3. Soak cucumber in the brine for 24 hours
4. Drain thoroughly then pack tightly into jars
5. Pour hot spiced vinegar to cover and seal in screwtop jars

Substitution: Free

PICKLED ONIONS

2 kg (4 lb) small white onions
½ cup salt
Liquid sweetener to taste
15 g (½ oz) mixed allspice
5 cups white vinegar

METHOD

1. Peel onions and put into a basin
2. Sprinkle with salt and leave to stand overnight
3. Rinse them thoroughly and dry as well as possible
4. Put sweetener, salt, spices and vinegar into a saucepan and bring to the boil
5. Add onions, cover and boil briskly for 4–5 minutes, or until soft
6. Pour into bottles and cover with airtight lids

Substitution: Free

PICKLED RED CABBAGE

½ large red cabbage
Salt
Spiced vinegar (p. 129)

METHOD

1. Shred cabbage finely
2. Wash thoroughly and place shreds into a deep bowl and sprinkle with layers of salt
3. Leave for 24 hours. Wash and drain thoroughly
4. Pour hot spiced vinegar over cabbage and leave for a further 24 hours, stirring at intervals
5. Pack into jars and cover with airtight lids

Substitution: Free

PINEAPPLE AND GRAPEFRUIT SALAD

2 cups diced pineapple
½ cup diced grapefruit
2 or 3 sprigs mint, chopped
2 tablespoons chopped green pepper (optional)

METHOD

1. Mix pineapple, grapefruit, mint and green pepper
2. Chill mixture for at least 1 hour before serving

Substitution: 1 portion fruit   Serves 4

RICE SALAD

2 cups cooked rice
½ cup finely sliced celery
¼ cup grated onion
¼ cup chopped radish
2 tablespoons chopped mint
2 teaspoons salt
¼ teaspoon pepper

METHOD

1. Combine all ingredients. Chill

Substitution: 30 g (1 oz) bread   Serves 4

TOMATO SALAD

¼ cup vinegar
¼ cup water
1 teaspoon caraway seeds
Salt and pepper
2 cups sliced tomato
½ cup sliced onion

METHOD

Combine vinegar, water, caraway seeds, salt and pepper
and pour over tomato and onion. Chill

Substitution: Free

DESSERTS

APPLE MILK JELLY

2 teaspoons gelatine
30 ml (1 fl oz) hot water
Liquid sweetener to taste
2½ cups skim milk
1 cup unsweetened apple purée

METHOD

1. Dissolve gelatine in hot water

2. Add artificial sweetener to apple purée
3. Mix skim milk with apple and gelatine
4. Refrigerate to set   Serves 4

Substitution: 1 portion fruit; 150 ml (5 fl oz) skim milk

BAKED APPLE

4 medium cooking apples
Spice
Cloves
Liquid sweetener to taste
Lemon juice

METHOD

1. Core apples. Place a couple of cloves and spices in centre of each apple
2. Place apples in baking dish with water, sweetener, lemon juice and bake slowly until tender, basting occasionally

Substitution: 1 portion fruit   Serves 4

VARIATION

Pears or nectarines may be substituted for apples

FRUIT SALAD

1 medium orange
1 medium diced apple
1 small sliced banana
½ cup diced pineapple
1 passionfruit, peach or pear

METHOD

Mix all fruit. Chill

Substitution: 1 portion fruit   Serves 4

JELLIED APPLE SNOW

250 g (8 oz) unsweetened apple purée
4 tablespoons water
Liquid sweetener to taste

Squeeze lemon juice
1 tablespoon gelatine
2 egg whites

METHOD

1. Soften gelatine in a little hot water and add to cooked apple
2. Cool. Fold in stiffly beaten egg whites
3. Turn into serving dish and allow to set

Substitution: 1 portion fruit   Serves 4

JELLIED PEACHES

4 medium peaches or 375 g (12 oz) drained
unsweetened canned fruit
1¼ cups diabetic jelly

METHOD

1. Distribute fruit evenly in dish
2. Pour in jelly and set

Substitution: 1 portion fruit   Serves 4

VARIATIONS

Any variety of unsweetened canned fruit or fresh fruit may be substituted for peaches. Use quantity equivalent to 4 serves

JUNKET

2 cups water
⅓ cup dried skim milk powder
Liquid sweetener to taste
2 junket tablets
2 teaspoons vanilla essence

METHOD

1. Warm milk to blood heat
2. Crush junket tablets and dissolve in a little water
3. Add crushed junket tablets, sweetener, vanilla to skim milk and pour into dish, sprinkle with nutmeg
4. Stand aside to set

Substitution: 150 ml (5 fl oz) skim milk   Serves 4

(see variation over page)

VARIATION

Coffee: Add 1 tablespoon powdered instant coffee to skim milk

MOCHA SPONGE

2 teaspoons gelatine
¼ cup water
¾ cup boiling coffee
Liquid sweetener to taste
2 egg whites

METHOD

1. Soften gelatine in water
2. Add coffee and sweetener and stir until dissolved
3. Leave until slightly thickened and then add stiffly beaten egg whites. Whisk until foamy. Chill

Substitution: Free   Serves 4

VARIATION

Flummery: Substitute 1 cup diluted calorie-free cordial for water and coffee

ORANGE AND PINEAPPLE DELIGHT

1 cup unsweetened pineapple pieces plus liquid
1 tablespoon gelatine
1 orange peeled and cut into segments
100 ml (3 fl oz) orange juice
100 ml (3 fl oz) cold water
2 tablespoons lemon juice
Liquid sweetener to taste

METHOD

1. Drain pineapple juice and soak gelatine in it
2. Bring orange juice and water to boil, add to gelatine, stir till dissolved. Add lemon juice and sweetener
3. Chill until setting then add pineapple and orange segments
4. Chill until set

Substitution: 1 portion fruit   Serves 4

ORANGE CREAM

1⅓ cups orange juice
1 tablespoon gelatine
Liquid sweetener to taste
⅓ cup non-fat milk powder
¼ cup iced water

METHOD

1. Dissolve gelatine in hot juice
2. Add sweetener, stir well and set aside to chill until the mixture begins to set
3. Sprinkle milk powder on iced water and beat until stiff
4. Fold into gelatine mixture and chill until set

Substitution: 1 portion fruit; 150 ml (5 fl oz) skim milk

Serves 4

PINEAPPLE DESSERT

2 teaspoons gelatine
1½ cups unsweetened pineapple pieces. Reserve juice
Liquid sweetener to taste
¼ teaspoon grated lemon rind
1 teaspoon vanilla
2 teaspoons lemon juice
Salt
1 cup skim milk

METHOD

1. Drain pineapple. Reserve pineapple juice and make up to ½ cup with water
2. Sprinkle gelatine into pineapple juice
3. Allow to stand 5 minutes then dissolve over gentle heat
4. Remove and stir in sweetener, lemon rind, vanilla, lemon juice, skim milk and drained pineapple. Chill

Substitution: 1 portion fruit   Serves 4

PINEAPPLE MINT SHERBERT

2 teaspoons gelatine
½ cup water

1 cup unsweetened juice
125 g (4 oz) unsweetened canned pineapple pieces
1 tablespoon chopped fresh mint
2 teaspoons lemon juice
2 egg whites
Liquid sweetener to taste

METHOD

1. Soften gelatine in water then add pineapple juice and pineapple, heat till gelatine has dissolved
2. Allow to cool, add chopped mint and lemon juice
3. Chill 1 hour
4. Beat egg whites till stiff and fold carefully through pineapple mixture. Sweeten if desired
5. Pour into wetted mould and allow to chill until firm

Substitution: 1 portion fruit   Serves 4

SAUCES AND DRESSINGS

CURRIED SAUCE

2 teaspoons curry powder
1 cup sliced onion
½ cup sliced green peppers
1 clove crushed garlic
1 tablespoon chopped green ginger or
1 teaspoon ground ginger
Juice of 1 lemon
2 cups tomato juice

METHOD

1. Heat pan; add curry and heat for few minutes
2. Add peppers, garlic, ginger, lemon juice and tomato juice and simmer gently till vegetables are soft

Substitution: Free

Use for curried meats. Pour over prepared meats, bake in moderate oven until meat is tender

MINT SAUCE

2 tablespoons hot water
2 tablespoons finely chopped mint
1 teaspoon liquid sweetener
3 tablespoons vinegar

METHOD

1. Pour hot water over mint, add sweetener and vinegar
2. Stir and set aside until cold

Substitution: Free

SPICED DRESSING

1 tablespoon water
3 tablespoons tarragon vinegar
1 tablespoon finely chopped chives
1 tablespoon chopped parsley
$\frac{1}{2}$ teaspoon salt
$\frac{1}{4}$ teaspoon pepper
$\frac{1}{2}$ teaspoon paprika
$\frac{1}{4}$ teaspoon oregano
Squeeze lemon juice

METHOD

1. Mix ingredients
2. Chill in refrigerator to blend flavours
3. Stir before serving

Substitution: Free

SPICED VINEGAR FOR PICKLING

1 tablespoon blade mace
1 tablespoon allspice
1 tablespoon cloves
$\frac{1}{4}$ stick cinnamon
6 peppercorns
$4\frac{1}{2}$ cups vinegar
Liquid sweetener to taste

METHOD

1. Tie all the spices in a muslin bag
2. Pour the vinegar into a saucepan. Add spices
3. Cover the pan and bring the vinegar slowly to the boil
4. Simmer for a few minutes, remove the pan from the stove, add sweetener and leave to stand 1 hour
5. Lift out the spice bag
6. The vinegar is ready for immediate use if required

Substitution: Free   Makes $4\frac{1}{2}$ cups

TOMATO CHUTNEY

2 kg (4 lb) ripe tomatoes
2 chopped green peppers
4 chopped chillies
$1\frac{1}{2}$ cups chopped celery
$1\frac{1}{2}$ cups chopped onion
Liquid sweetener to taste
2 teaspoons Tabasco sauce
1 tablespoon salt
$1\frac{1}{2}$ cups cider vinegar
1 stick cinnamon
1 teaspoon whole cloves
$1\frac{1}{2}$ teaspoons mustard seed
$1\frac{1}{2}$ teaspoons celery seed

METHOD

1. Pour boiling water over tomatoes to loosen skin. Peel and chop
2. In large saucepan combine tomatoes, green peppers, chillies, celery, onion, liquid sweetener, Tabasco, salt and vinegar
3. Tie spices in muslin bag and add to tomato mixture
4. Bring to the boil
5. Reduce heat and simmer, stirring occasionally until of desired consistency (approximately 2 hours)
6. Remove muslin bag. Pour into hot sterilized jars. Seal at once

Substitution: Free   Makes 4 cups

TOMATO DRESSING

1 tin tomato juice
Juice of 1 lemon
8 tablespoons white vinegar
2 cloves crushed garlic
1 tablespoon finely chopped chives
3–4 drops Tabasco sauce

METHOD
1. Combine all ingredients, shake well and chill
2. Store in refrigerator

Substitution: Free

TOMATO SAUCE

3 kg (6 lb) tomatoes
500 g (1 lb) onions
15 g ($\frac{1}{2}$ oz) garlic
90 g (3 oz) salt
15 g ($\frac{1}{2}$ oz) cloves
15 g ($\frac{1}{2}$ oz) ground ginger
1$\frac{1}{4}$ cups vinegar

METHOD
1. Chop tomatoes and onions roughly
2. Add chopped garlic, salt, cloves and ground ginger tied in muslin
3. Boil gently about 2 hours
4. Strain into saucepan, add vinegar and simmer until thick
5. Bottle and seal

Substitution: Free

YOGHURT SALAD DRESSING

1 clove crushed garlic
1 teaspoon mustard
1 teaspoon paprika
1 tablespoon vinegar
250 g (8 oz) plain low fat yoghurt

METHOD

1. Mix garlic, mustard and paprika with vinegar
2. Mix thoroughly with yoghurt
3. Let stand 2 hours before using

Substitution: 1 tablespoon free

ZERO SALAD DRESSING

1 cup tomato juice
3 tablespoons lemon juice
2 tablespoons finely chopped onion
¼ teaspoon pepper

METHOD

1. Mix all ingredients
2. Store in refrigerator
3. Shake before using

Substitution: Free

BEVERAGES

LEMON TINGLE

Ice cubes
Juice of 4 lemons
1 teaspoon powdered ginger or sliced green ginger
2 large bottles soda water
Liquid sweetener to taste

METHOD

1. Place ice cubes in jug
2. Add lemon, powdered ginger and soda water
3. Mix well and serve immediately

Substitution: Free   Serves 4

SPARKLING MINT TEA

2 cups strong tea
Liquid sweetener to taste
½ cup lemon juice
1 cup soda water (chilled)
Mint, ice

1. Strain tea, add liquid sweetener
2. Let stand until cold
3. Stir in lemon juice, add soda water and serve in tall glasses with ice, mint and lemon slices

Substitution: Free   Makes $3\frac{1}{2}$ cups

SPICED TEA

$\frac{1}{8}$ *teaspoon grated nutmeg*
$\frac{1}{8}$ *teaspoon ground allspice*
$\frac{1}{8}$ *teaspoon ground cinnamon*
2 cups hot water
1 tablespoon tea
$\frac{1}{4}$ *cup orange juice*
$\frac{1}{4}$ *cup lemon juice*
2 cups cold water
Liquid sweetener to taste

METHOD

1. Tie spices securely in muslin bag, add hot water, boil 1 minute
2. Pour over tea leaves and steep 3 minutes
3. Strain, then add fruit juices and cold water. Chill
4. Add liquid sweetener according to taste and serve very cold

Substitution: Free   Makes $4\frac{1}{2}$ cups

TOMATO COOLER

$1\frac{1}{2}$ *cups tomato juice*
$\frac{1}{4}$ *cup finely chopped celery*
2 teaspoons soy sauce
2 drops Tabasco sauce
1 tablespoon lemon juice

METHOD

1. Combine all ingredients, add salt to taste if desired
2. Chill until ready to serve

Substitution: Free   Serves 2

MENU FROM AUSTRALIA FOR ENERGY RESTRICTED DIET, DIET NO. 1

(See also p. 98)

	BREAKFAST	LUNCH	DINNER
SUNDAY	Fruit juice (1PV) Cereal (1B) and milk Scrambled egg Toast (1B)	Roast leg lamb mint sauce (129) Roast potato (117) (1PV) Roast pumpkin (117) (1PV) Broccoli Pineapple dessert (127) (1PF)	Salmon and tomato savoury (109) Rice (1B) Fresh fruit (1PF)
MONDAY	Cereal (1B) and milk 1 poached egg Toast (1B)	Cold lamb slices Coleslaw (120) zero dressing (132) Asparagus Bread (1B) Fresh fruit (1PF) **or** Packed lunch as above	Braised rabbit (114) Boiled potato (2PV) Brussels sprouts (1PV) Savoury stuffed tomato (118) Jellied apple snow (124) (1PF)
TUESDAY	Tomato juice Cape Cod, lemon wedges Toast (1B)	1 cheese and lettuce sandwich (2B) Celery curls Fresh fruit (2PF) **or** Packed lunch as above	Grilled steak Mashed potato (1PV) Carrot straws (1PV) Cauliflower and parsley Orange and pineapple delight (126) (1PF = 1PV)
WEDNESDAY	½ grapefruit 1 boiled egg Toast (1B)	Soused fish (110) Tossed salad Wholemeal bread (2B) Fresh fruit (1PF) **or** Packed lunch 1 salmon and celery sandwich (2B) 1 fresh fruit (1PF)	Hawaiian chicken (116) (1PF = 1PV) Boiled rice (1B = 2PV) Beans Junket (125) Unsweetened canned apricots (1PF)

THURSDAY

Pineapple juice (1PV)
1 poached egg
Toast (1B)

Chinese chicken soup (107)
Cottage cheese
Rice salad (123) (1B) yoghurt salad
  dressing (131)
Tomato salad (123)
Lettuce
Wholemeal bread (1B)
Fresh fruit (1PF)
or
Packed lunch as above

Steak Diane (113)
Baked jacket potato (1PV)
Lima beans (1PV)
Cauliflower
Orange cream (127) (1PF)

FRIDAY

Cereal (1B) and milk
Grilled cheese toast (1B)

1 stuffed curried egg
Sardines
Celery curls, cucumber, tomato
Bread (1B)
Fresh fruit (1PF + 1PV)
or
Packed lunch as above

Corned silverside
Mashed potato (1PV)
Carrots (1PV)
Onions
Fresh fruit salad (124) (2PF)

SATURDAY

Tomato omelette
Toast (2B)

Cold corned beef slices
Coleslaw (120), spiced dressing
  (129)
Cucumber and onion salad
Wholemeal bread (1B)
Fresh fruit (1PF)

Celery soup (106)
Marinaded baked fish (109) lemon
  wedges
Parsley steamed potato (1PV)
Peas (2PV)
Flummery (126)
Unsweetened canned peaches
  (1PF)

1PV = equivalent to 1 portion of starchy vegetable
1PF = equivalent to 1 portion of fruit
1B = equivalent to 30 g (1 oz) bread

Menu items marked with one of the above symbols show how the use of substitutions can add variety to your diet.

MENU FROM AUSTRALIA FOR ENERGY RESTRICTED DIET, DIET NO. 2

(See also p. 98)

	BREAKFAST	LUNCH	DINNER
SUNDAY	Pineapple juice (1PF = 1PV) Cereal (1B) skim milk Stewed tomato and onion Toast (1B)	Celery soup (106) Roast chicken Roast potato (117) (1PV) Roast pumpkin (117) (1PV) Beans Orange and pineapple delight (126) (1PF)	Meat sauce (112) and spaghetti (1B) Tossed salad and tarragon dressing (82) (O) Fresh fruit (1PF)
MONDAY	Cereal (1B) skim milk Asparagus Toast (1B)	Cold chicken Rice salad (123) (1B) yoghurt salad dressing (131) Tomato slices, lettuce Fresh fruit (1PF) **or** Packed lunch as above	Grilled fish (31) (O) lemon wedges Mashed potato (2PV) Corn (1PV) Broccoli Mocha sponge (126) Unsweetened canned pears (1PF)
TUESDAY	Tomato juice Corn niblets (1PV) Toast (1B)	Quick salmon snack (109) Coleslaw (120) piquant sauce (81) (O) Wholemeal bread (2B) Fresh fruit (1PF) **or** Packed lunch 1 salmon and cucumber sandwich (2B) Coleslaw (120) piquant sauce (81) (O) Fresh fruit (1PF)	Corned leg of mutton Potato (1PV) Carrot (1PV) Cabbage Pineapple and mint sherbert (127) (1PF)
WEDNESDAY	Grapefruit Cereal (1B) and 'filled milk' (85) (O)	Corned mutton slices Green bean ring (120) Radishes, lettuce	Julienne soup (107) Veal Marengo (114) Poppy seed macaroni (2PV)

Toast (1B)

Bread (1B)
Fresh fruit (1PF)
or
Packed lunch as above (omit Bean ring)

Peas (1PV)
Cauliflower
Flummery (126)
Unsweetened canned apricots (1PF)

THURSDAY

Orange juice (1PF)
Cereal (1B) and 'filled milk' (8s) (O)
Toast (1B)

Salmon and tomato savoury (109)
Celery
Wholemeal bread (1B)
Fresh fruit (1PF)
or
Packed lunch
Salmon
Celery, tomato, asparagus
Wholemeal bread (1B)
Fresh fruit (1PF)

Braised chops (111)
Baked jacket potato (1PV)
Pumpkin (1PV)
Spinach
Jellied fruit (125) (1PF = 1PV)

FRIDAY

Grapefruit
Cape Cod and lemon wedges
Toast (1B)

Cottage cheese and walnut (O)
Radish, tomato, lettuce
Fresh fruit (1PF)
Bread (2B)
or
Packed lunch as above

Baked fish (108)
Mashed potato (2PV)
Carrot straws (1PV)
Beans
Baked apple (124) (1PF)

SATURDAY

Cereal (1B) skim milk
Corn niblets with tomato (1PV)
Toast (1B)

Asparagus soup (106)
Mexican rice (113) (1B) (O)
Salad and spiced dressing (129)
Fresh fruit (1PF)

Curried rabbit (128)
Tomato chutney (130)
Mashed potato (1PV)
Peas (1PV)
Marrow + chopped parsley
Jellied apple snow (124) (1PF)

1PV = equivalent to 1 portion of starchy vegetable
O = equivalent to 15 ml ($\frac{1}{2}$ fl oz) polyunsaturated oil
1PF = equivalent to 1 portion of fruit
1B = equivalent to 30 g (1 oz) bread

Menu items marked with one of the above symbols show how the use of substitutions can add variety to your diet.

9
GLOSSARY OF
MEDICAL TERMS

Adipose tissue: Fatty tissue

Alcohol: Alcohol is produced by yeast fermentation of sugar or starchy materials and yields a solution of approximately 19% alcohol at which strength the alcohol kills off the yeast. It has an energy value of 7 Calories per gram. The energy content of the usual amounts served of some alcoholic beverages is:

300 ml (10 fl oz) beer = 115 Calories
  30 ml (1 fl oz) spirit = 70 Calories (whisky, gin, brandy, rum, vodka)
150 ml (5 fl oz) champagne = 125 Calories
180 ml (6½ fl oz) fermented cider = 70 Calories
  20 ml (⅔ fl oz) liqueur = 70 Calories
Wines 60 ml (2 fl oz) dry sherry, vermouth = 70 Calories
        60 ml (2 fl oz) sweet sherry, sweet vermouth, port, madeira = 85 Calories
        100 ml (3½ fl oz) red, white wine = 85 Calories

Atherosclerosis: A disease in which there is a thickening and narrowing of the arteries, also referred to as 'hardening of the arteries'. The mushy deposit of fat and cholesterol in the inner layer of the arterial wall interferes with the normal blood flow and nourishment of the tissues. It predisposes to heart attacks and strokes

Basal metabolic rate: The rate at which energy is used in maintaining the functions of the body when it is at complete rest.

Calorie: A unit of heat energy also used to express food energy values.

Carbohydrates: Substances such as sugars, starch, cellulose. Carbohydrates liberate an average of 4 Calories per gram (114 per ounce) when oxidized to carbon dioxide and water.

Cellulose: Complex carbohydrate that forms the supporting cell structure in plants. It is not digested in man, but provides bulk for intestinal functioning.

Cholesterol: A waxy substance with fat-like properties widely present in animal tissues, and therefore in most foods of animal origin. It can also be manufactured by the body. Rich sources of cholesterol are egg yolk, liver, brains, kidney, fish roe.

Coronary heart disease: The most common form of adult heart disease in which the main arteries of the heart (the coronary arteries) are affected by atherosclerosis and thrombosis and the flow of blood through them is impaired. There are different forms of the disease and different names for it – angina pectoris, ischaemic heart disease, myocardial infarction.

Energy: Defined as the ability to do work. The body requires energy for muscular activity, to maintain body temperature and to carry out metabolic processes. This energy comes from the oxidation of nutrients – carbohydrates, fats and such protein as is surplus to tissue-building requirements. It may also be obtained from alcohol. Energy is stored in the body, chemically, as fat.

Fats: Compounds of glycerol with fatty acids. Oils are fats which are liquid at room temperature. They are the most concentrated form of energy, providing 9 Calories per gram (256 per ounce).

Fatty acids: A major component of 'fats'. They are generally classified as saturated and unsaturated.

Fibre: Refers to the indigestible organic tissue, particularly cellulose.

Hydrogenation: A process whereby unsaturated fat is converted to saturated fat by the addition of hydrogen to the molecule.

Lipids: Fat-like substances which are soluble in alcohol, benzine and similar solvents but not in water. They include triglycerides and cholesterol.

Metabolic rate: Rate of utilization of energy. Increased by anxiety, digestive action or physical activity. Metabolic rate includes basal metabolic rate plus any extra energy spent on other activities.

Metabolism: The chemical processes that go on in living cells – growth of new tissue, breakdown of old tissue, production of energy.

Mono-unsaturated fatty acids: Unsaturated fatty acids with one unsaturated bond in each molecule.

Nutrient: A substance which maintains growth and renewal of the tissues and organs. Proteins, fats, carbohydrates, minerals, vitamins and water are nutrients.

Nutrition: The combination of processes by which the living organism receives and utilizes nutrients.

Obesity: Excessive body fatness.

Polyunsaturated fatty acids: Unsaturated fatty acids with two or more unsaturated bonds in each molecule. Most vegetable oils, many nuts and fish fats are rich in polyunsaturated fatty acids.

Proteins: Essential constituents of all living cells. They provide 4 Calories per gram when oxidized.

Saccharine: An artificial sweetening agent 550 times as sweet as sucrose. It is unstable to heat and has no food value.

Saturated fatty acids: Fatty acids which are fully saturated with hydrogen. Fats in which saturated fatty acids predominate are referred to as saturated fats. They are usually solid and of animal origin.

Sorbitol: An artificial sweetening agent produced from six-carbon sugar alcohol formed by the reduction of fructose. It provides 4 Calories per gram when oxidized.

Starch: Complex carbohydrate composed of units of glucose. It is the form in which carbohydrate is stored in the plant.

Sucrose: A carbohydrate derived from cane sugar or beet sugar.

Sugar: Usually refers to sucrose or table sugar. Other sugars are milk sugar (lactose), fruit sugar (fructose), grape sugar (glucose), and malt sugar (maltose).

Thrombosis: Coagulation of blood in the blood vessels. The clot thus formed is termed a thrombus.

Triglycerides: The common form of fats, made up of three fatty acids attached to each molecule of glycerol.

Unsaturated fatty acids: Fatty acids which are not fully saturated with hydrogen. These may be either mono-unsaturated or polyunsaturated fatty acids.

INDEX TO RECIPES

(F)   *indicates recipe is suitable for Modified Fat Diet*
(C)   *indicates recipe is suitable for Calorie Restricted Diet*